JUMPST
STORYMAKING

The *Jumpstart!* books contain 'quick-fire' ideas that could be used as warm-ups and starters as well as possibly extended into lessons. There are more than 100 provocative games and activities for Key Stage 1, 2 or 3 classrooms. Practical, easy-to-do and vastly entertaining, the 'jumpstarts' will appeal to busy teachers in any primary or Key Stage 3 classroom.

Also available in the series:

Jumpstart! Literacy
Games and Activities for Ages 7–14
978-1-84312-102-2
Pie Corbett

Jumpstart! Poetry
Games and Activities for Ages 7–12
978-0-415-46708-7
Pie Corbett

Jumpstart! Creativity
Games and Activities for Ages 7–14
978-0-415-43273-7
Steve Bowkett

Jumpstart! ICT
ICT Activities and Games for Ages 7–14
978-1-84312-465-8
John Taylor

Jumpstart! Numeracy
Maths Activities and Games for Ages 5–14
978-1-84312-264-7
John Taylor

JUMPSTART!
STORYMAKING

GAMES AND ACTIVITIES FOR AGES 7–12

Pie Corbett

Routledge
Taylor & Francis Group

LONDON AND NEW YORK

First published 2009
by Routledge
2 Park Square, Milton Park, Abingdon, Oxon, OX14 4RN

Simultaneously published in the USA and Canada
by Routledge
711 Third Ave, New York, NY 10017

Routledge is an imprint of the Taylor & Francis Group, an informa business

British Library Cataloguing in Publication Data
A catalogue record for this book is available from the British Library.

Library of Congress Cataloging in Publication Data
Corbett, Pie.
Jumpstart! storymaking : games and activities for ages 7–12 / Pie Corbett.
 p. cm.
1. Literature–Study and teaching (Elementary)–Activity programs.
2. Literature–Study and teaching (Middle school)–Activity programs.
I. Title.
LB1575.C67 2009
372.64'044–dc22
                                                                        2008025170

ISBN 10: 0-415-46686-5 (pbk)
ISBN 10: 0-203-88339-X (ebk)

ISBN 13: 978-0-415-46686-8 (pbk)
ISBN 13: 978-0-203-88339-6 (ebk)

Typeset in Palatino/Scala Sans by FiSH Books, Enfield
Printed and bound in Great Britain by
CPI Antony Rowe, Chippenham, Wilts

Contents

Acknowledgements

A few examples of children's work in this book were first published in *My Grandmother's Motorcyle* by Pie Corbett and Brian Moses (Oxford University Press, 1991).

This book is dedicated to all those teachers who keep storytelling alive in their classrooms – especially the original teacher-researchers on the Storymaking Project, from whom I learned so much.

Some of the ideas for encouraging reading were originated by the National Literacy Trust which has played such a key role in promoting reading in schools and communities. My thanks to the Trust, and especially Julia Strong, for supporting 'storymaking' and providing me with the opportunity to share these ideas with thousands of teachers.

By word of mouth: the story of the story

Once, long ago, in a place that is neither here nor there but is everywhere, there was a time when trouble came to the land. But one man knew where to go in the forest. There he lit a fire, chanted the words, and so it was that disaster passed. Now he went and told the story in the market square about how disaster had been diverted, and thousands flocked to hear. So it was that by word of mouth the story was handed down.

Now the years ran by till, in the end, another threat appeared; and one man who had stood listening in that square all those years before remembered that he had to go into the forest, but he was not sure where. However, he lit a fire, chanted the words, and so it was that disaster passed. Now he, too, went and told the story in the market square about how disaster had been diverted, and hundreds came to listen. So it was that by word of mouth the story was passed down.

Now the years ran by until, in the end, another disaster, greater than before, threatened the world. And one man who had stood listening in that square all those years before did not know where to go nor did he know what to do, but he remembered to chant the words, and so it was that disaster passed. Now he went, too, and told the story in the market place about how disaster had been diverted, and a few people came to watch but all the others were too busy with their lives. So it was that by word of mouth the story was spoken.

Now the years ran by until in the end the worst of all possible threats appeared. And one man who sat in his house, twitching the curtains and watching the world rush by, remembered that something needed to be said and done. But he didn't know where to go, and he didn't know what to do, and he no longer knew the words. And so it was that the worst of all possible threats visited the land – for the story had disappeared. It had shrivelled and died on the tongues of woman and man all those years before.

No one listened. No one spoke. No one knew.

And that is why we need to listen to our story as it flows through the centuries by word of mouth.

Introduction

There have been great societies that did not use the wheel, but there have been no societies that did not tell stories.
Ursula K. LeGuin (1979) from *The Language of the Night: Essays on Fantasy and Science Fiction*

Storymaking began as an international research project based at the International Learning and Research Centre. The initial project was co-led by Mary Rose and myself. We set out to discover how to help children learn another language through storytelling. The idea was quite simple: the children would learn to tell a story in their own language and then learn the same story in another language.

One of the by-products of the teacher research was that the process improved the children's writing. The Education Department (then known as the DFES) then gave us money, through the 'Innovations Unit', to explore 'telling into writing'. This helped us work with teachers to develop storymaking across primary schools.

We taught the children stories orally, and when they knew them really well they innovated on the story, changing them to create something new. We also built in opportunities for children to make up their own stories. Over the following seven years, I gathered a range of storymaking games and activities that help develop children as storytellers and story writers as well as story readers and performers. This book is intended to provide a bank of story games to help children develop confidence and expertise in storymaking. It involves storytelling but also includes storywriting, story reading and dramatising as well as a round-up of ideas for developing a storytelling, story reading and storywriting culture in a school community.

Recent teacher research in Lewisham has showed impressive results with storymaking. The children involved made better progress in writing than in reading. One hundred per cent made progress of two sublevels in the year and 80 per cent made an impressive three sublevels. In other words, most of the children actually made two years' progress in one year. This sort of improvement has been noticed in many schools where teachers have had the chance to devote time and energy to thinking creatively and innovatively about what children need in order to develop as young tellers and writers. This approach to story creating lies at the heart of narrative teaching progression in the new English National Primary Framework. So what is 'storymaking'? How can we develop our own storytelling? How do we help children become storytellers? Storymaking has three strands.

IMITATION

Why is it that some children can make up stories so easily? The answer is that they have read so much (or been read to so much) that they have internalised the narrative patterns they need. Avid reading builds up a narrative storehouse of linguistic patterns and imagined possibilities that young writers draw upon. This explains why my stories, written when I was about 10 years old, all were adventures involving three children and a dog called Scamp! I read so much Enid Blyton. that I wrote Blytonese! So the challenge for teachers is how to help children build up and draw upon the narrative storehouse.

To help children internalise stories, set yourselves the task of learning by heart about ten stories in Foundation and year 1 – thereafter about one every half-term. This would give the children about 50 stories by the time they left the primary school. In key stage 1 this needs to be the daily telling of communal stories – as regular as phonics or action rhymes and songs.

To learn the stories communally, they need to be told orally with the children increasingly joining in until they can retell the whole story. Once they know it really well, then they can move from telling as a whole class to story circles and finally to working in pairs. To help the children remember the stories, actions can be used to depict events or to emphasise language features such as connectives. A storymap provides a strong visual reminder.

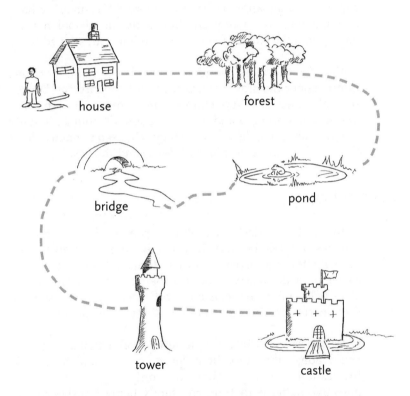

Other activities can be provided such as drama, model-making, painting, discussion, baking gingerbread men and growing beans. All these help the children understand the story and make it memorable.

This daily routine helps children begin to build a set of stories that they know really well. These would include such obvious tales as 'The Little Red Hen', 'The Gingerbread Man' and 'The Billy Goats Gruff'. Gradually, stories from other cultures can also be stirred into the story pot. Learning the stories word for word is no hardship to the children. It is the same as chanting, 'The Farmer's in His Den'. Actually, it replicates what all children do if they are told stories at home. They move through a phase when they demand the same story again and again until they know it word for word. Of course, we have to remember that many children arrive in school not yet having had the chance to become familiar with a loved tale.

With older and more confident storytellers, you do not have to remember the stories word for word. A story can be told several times and the children may move straight into drawing a storymap and retelling pairs. Of course, initially their retellings will lack flow so they will need to retell at least three or four times to gain confidence and fluency.

INNOVATION

Actually, the easiest part of this process is the children learning to retell the story. It seems that they have an endless capacity for internalising stories. Indeed, they will find it easier than the teacher because their brains are still at the stage of learning language. It is worth loitering with a story so that the children become very familiar with its patterns.

Once the story is in the long-term working memory, they could adapt the story in order to create something new. Interestingly enough, there are only a few underlying narrative patterns that are constantly being transposed and interwoven. Look carefully at the tale of *Beowulf* and compare it to *Jaws* – in essence, they are the same story. Both involve a monster coming out of the watery depths. Both stories need a hero to conquer the monster.

Small children and those to whom English is a new language begin with simple substitutions. They retell their story but might alter characters, places and simple objects. In this way, it feels to them like a new story. Lead the children through the process by redrawing a new storymap and including changes that you make. As you do this, take the children through the same process so that you end up with a new class version – and every child has their own variation. They should then develop and rehearse their stories in pairs before recording them.

Older children could retell their story with embellishments or alterations. Characters, settings and key events could be changed – suspense or action might be developed, descriptions built up, endings altered, viewpoint changed or an old tale modernised. Time needs to be taken over innovations so that new maps or storyboards can be drawn and changes gradually added into the children's retellings. With older pupils, shared and independent writing is an opportunity to slow down the story and draw upon reading, further crafting the tale.

INVENTION

The third strand is the ability to invent or make up a story. This needs very regular practice. If Barbara Hardy was right in claiming that 'narrative is a primary act of mind' then all of us are constantly engaged in making stories out of our lives. We predict the story of our future and recast our past in narrative format. It is through story that we shape ourselves and communicate – through gossip, anecdote and chit-chat to news, TV and radio. Our brains are constantly making stories in order to explain the world to ourselves and ourselves to the world. So storymaking has to be an integral part of daily education. If you listen to effective teachers they make everything sound like a story. They do not just impart information; they dress it up in story form. This is a powerful and effective teaching method.

In Foundation, year 1 and 2, it is helpful if once a week the class can have at least one whole-class story invention session. This need not take long. In many classes, children like this so much that they demand a storymaking session every day. They even arrive ready with ideas.

As long as the teacher has in mind a simple pattern to guide the tale, the process is easy enough. You can just make a story up orally or write one down as you invent on a notepad or flip chart. Some teachers like to draw a storymap or storyboard as the tale is created.

Younger children also need plenty of fun opportunities to play at storymaking – sand trays, fuzzy felt, finger puppets, story boxes and castles where story play can occur. It is simple enough to stand around the sand tray with some models. Dampen the sand and draw a pathway. Now make up a little tale about travelling from one place to another and meeting animals on the way. Leave the models with the children so that they can then make up their own sand stories.

Older pupils also need practise in developing their narrative voice. Many of the games in this book provide ideas for developing stories, characters, exploring settings and creating dilemmas. Older pupils may find using the story mountain pattern helpful. As they grow in confidence they should manipulate the basic pattern.

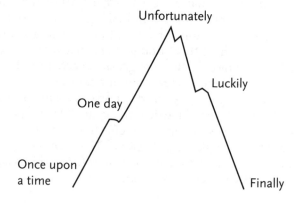

Key connective	Story intention
Once upon a time	Introduce a character in a setting
One day	The story begins – the main charter starts to do something
Unfortunately	Something goes wrong
Luckily	It gets sorted out
Finally	Everything ends alright

This book provides mini games and activities that will support a school or department that is establishing storymaking as a process across the school. The ability to tell a story arises out of building up and drawing upon a bank of well-known tales. The best writers in a class are always avid readers drawing upon the narrative storehouse. Strugglers may have not yet built up that storehouse so they are unfamiliar with the images and language patterns. Some teachers feel that their children are 'unimaginative'. The problem for many is not so much to do with a *lack* of imagination but rather a lack of the building blocks with which to *be* imaginative. Storymaking provides those building blocks.

Finally, storytelling is often viewed as a young child's domain. Everyone expects to find stories in infant classrooms but by secondary school some believe that children should have moved away from such childish matters. Sadly, such a view is enshrined in the curriculum for older pupils – storytelling is somehow seen as a sub-species of story writing. But the writing can only arise out of the telling – even if the telling happens silently inside the writer's head.

Storytelling is a highly sophisticated activity that helps children develop their auditory memory, communication skills and imaginative world, and to manipulate language to create effects. It is crucial for all those who struggle with the written word because it makes writing easier and, more importantly, it provides extended, abstract thought.

But stories are also experiences. They lie at the heart of all cultures and their power is the story itself. We can discuss a story, deepening our understanding and appreciation. Ultimately, it is crucial to have the story learnt by heart so that it becomes part of who we are. Good stories change the brain forever. They enlarge who we are, taking us into uncharted territories and broadening our experience. From the urban legend to Gilgamesh, storytelling should be a necessity for every pupil at secondary school. It is not merely for infants and juniors.

NB: Many of the games need cards of characters, settings, dilemmas, props and so forth. In the resources section, I have listed various storymaking resources – though, of course, you could make you own.

CHAPTER 1

Creative warm-ups

Many of the quick-fire games that teachers use as 'lesson starters' have a very obvious educational intent. They are there to develop spelling or the ability to create and manipulate sentences. These games are just to warm up thinking, creating a lively atmosphere with everyone engaged. It is worth modelling the games before playing them. I also find it helpful to have a pair or group play the game in front of everyone.

GUESSING GAME

The children work in pairs. One child thinks of – an animal, famous person, place, type of food, etc. The partner has to discover what it is by asking questions to which the answers can only be 'yes', 'no' or 'maybe'. Only ten questions can be asked. You may need to increase the number of questions if ten is found to be generally insufficient.

AVOIDING SAYING A LETTER GAME

The players of the game have to role play, talk on a topic or tell a story, but they must avoid using a certain letter, e.g. 's'. This has the effect of making them watch their words a bit. If it is too easy, ask the children to talk a little faster. Soon enough, someone will trip up. Use a timer to see who lasts the longest.

The written version of the game is to rewrite a current pop song, nursery rhyme, traditional rhyme or short poem that has been provided without using a common letter, such as 'e'.

SPEED WRITING

To warm up the brain and get into a creative mood give the children a topic and ask them to write as much as they can in, say, one minute. Time them and ask them to count the number of words, then try again with another topic. They should write as rapidly as possible. This limbers and frees up the mind. They should concentrate on capturing the flow of words rather than worrying about spelling or handwriting. Surprisingly, this can sometimes produce rather good pieces of writing – often superior to those that have been laboured over for twenty minutes under duress.

SPEED CHINESE WHISPERS

The class stands in teams of equal numbers. Give a slip of paper with a sentence written on it to the child at the end of each team. On the word 'go', they have to whisper the sentence to the next down the line. The sentence is passed on in this way as fast as possible until it reaches the front. The winning team is the fastest and the team that also gets the closest approximation to the original sentence. Tongue twisters are fun to use!

VIDEO WRITING

Play a video or film track with the sound turned down. The children use this as a basis for writing as rapidly as possible – the story of what is happening; a description; or just anything that the images trigger. It has to be fast with no pauses. If they get stuck, just look up at what is happening and launch in again. There is no right or wrong; the only wrong thing is if you stop writing. Who can write the most words down?

MAKING LINKS

Randomly select two things – objects work well. Let us say that you have chosen the Moon and a car. On a board draw two circles like a pair of eyes spread wide apart. Put a word inside each eye. Now brainstorm ideas for ways in which they are linked. Draw a line and annotate each link, e.g. *car wheels are the same shape as the Moon*. Ask the children to make as many connections as possible. The winner of the game is the child or pair with the most connections.

STARBOARD

All writers are interested in words. I own a number of dictionaries of word and phrase origins. I was looking through Linda and Roger Flavell's *Dictionary of Word Orgins* when this little game occurred to me. I was on the page that explains how the word starboard came into being and it drew my attention because I had been thinking about skateboards. I wondered if I could invent different 'boards', e.g. moonboard, sunboard, cloudboard, swimboard, tearboard, rainboard, windowboard.

Next time I was in school, I provided a list of compound words and asked the children to split them, select ten openings randomly and ten different endings and then to create new words – plus their definitions. So starboard and stepchild and tadpole might provide:

- starpole – the short pole that is a form of telescope. It points at a star and a small screen shows all the details about it.
- stepboard – a moveable step made out of a board.
- tadchild – small child.

Try using the following compound words:

Blindfold	Buttonhole	Firecracker	Scapegoat
Bonfire	Cartoon	Kidnap	Snapdragon
Budget	Coconut	Magpie	Sunday
Bugbear	Cowslip	Masterpiece	Unwanted
Bullfrog	Deadline	Nightmare	Uproar
Butterfly	Earwig	Sandwich	Voiceless

PATTERN SPOTTING

Searching for patterns is an important brain activity. As human beings we exist through patterns of behaviour that help us cope with the world. Try any game where children have to find a pattern or spot where it is broken. This might be a list of words that rhyme and spotting the one that does not within ten seconds:

> Rough, Tough, Enough, Bluff, Cuff
> Through, Duff, Dough, Fluff, Gruff, Stuff

Identifying the underlying patterns in sentences is important and quite demanding. Try listing three examples that follow the same pattern and then ask the children to imitate and come up with the same pattern themselves, e.g.:

> Before Donni sang, everyone hoped he would keep in tune.
> While Donni was singing, everyone put their hands over their ears.
> After Donni finished singing, everyone cheered with relief.

Try using just one sentence and ask them to write it out and then, directly below, imitate it, e.g.:

> As they came to the last tree in the row, where the field ended, Mrs Wentleberry halted, wondering whether she should climb all the way to the top.

As they reached the corner shop, where the road curved left, Mr Snaggletooth stopped, hoping there would be some jelly babies left.

As he ran down the hill, where the stream trickled, Johnson paused, expecting there would be at least one tunnel into the hillside.

As with all things – start simply, e.g.:

Angrily, he stormed out of the room.
Happily, she whistled a tune.
Gleefully, he ate the doughnuts.
Unfortunately, she had one too many.

NEW EXPERIENCES

The brain is stimulated by new experiences – it makes us curious and generates language. First-hand experience makes brains grow. Each weekend, try looking for something curious that you could take into the classroom – photos, a mirror, a key, a Salvador Dali picture, an old watch, a gnarled piece of bark. Use these for rapid drawing and writing. To write, you could just brainstorm words and ideas as a class or individually in a few minutes. What does it look like/remind you of? What do associate with this? What might it be used for? Invent five new things you could use it for. What might a martian think it was?

Keep your ongoing collection of curious items in a 'writing box'. Let the children take any angle they wish. Steven, aged 7, wrote this short piece about an old watch that I popped in:

THE SILVER WATCH

The back is smooth and round. It has hinges to open it. It has a gold wheel that spins round. It has springs. The spring beats out and in like a heart. It has a silver plate with patterns. The patterns are curls. The best part I like is the gold colour inside. The time is quarter past six. That is all I know of the silver watch.

Deborah, aged 8 years, wrote about a small box and the unicorn that it contained.

What has the box ever held? A diamond? A ring? A heart of rubies? Or a unicorn with a sapphire collar? The inside of the box is as black as ebony. The unicorn can never feel happy or sad. The unicorn is trapped between both, never will he move again. The person who owned the box was a merchant who staggered around. The merchant rode a golden camel. The box was his favourite possession. Yet only he knew what it contained. He passed on the secret to me. Inside the box was a key, a key to let the soul of the unicorn out into the world . . .

PLAYFUL WRITING

The brain develops when it has to play hard at working. Being playful with ideas and language engages the prefrontal cortex and develops our highest cognitive functions. Novelty and innovation are important for brain growth. Whilst routines help to organise, regiment and make sure that children feel safe and confident, they also need new experiences and to develop creative thought. This demands training the brain to think in different ways so that it can generate ideas and possibilities, moving beyond what is expected.

The old magic box game is great fun and never ever fails. Everyone should be armed with a copy of Kit Wright's poems. Macmillan will be publishing a complete collection soon, but meanwhile, you need a copy of *Cat among the Pigeons*, which contains his poem 'The Magic Box'. All you have to do is imagine what might be in there – the poem is a great model for stimulating ideas. It can help to discuss what might be in a box first. Then make a class list (the quicker and the longer, the better) of things that would be impossible to have in a box – sunsets, a universe, a star, a rhino, a playground, a dream, a memory, a lie, a kangaroo, a rainbow, a scream, etc. Now just make an embellished list:

In the box of impossibilities you will find –
a sunset of crimson and gold,
a universe of whirling minds,
a shivering star,
a charging rhino with skin of metal,
a playground rumour
a daydream that comes alive,
a memory of a moment that was cold,
a lie like a nettle sting. . .

Older children should perhaps create a box of disasters or hatred so that they can dump all the bad things that clutter up their lives! A good source for other playful ideas would be *The Works: Poems for Key Stage 2* edited by Pie Corbett (Macmillan Children's Books). In the anthology there are plenty of poetry ideas that have a playful element. Most of the ideas could be used well into key stages 3 or 4. Many more such ideas are found in the companion volume to this book, *Jumpstart! Poetry*. It is worth remembering that play lies at the heart of storymaking – stories are playful, though often truthful, representations of experience. When you go to the theatre you watch a 'play'.

DISASTERS

Children – indeed most humans – are fascinated by disasters. But what might be a disaster for superman or an ant?

Five Disasters for Superman

1. His tights are in the wash.
2. The colour in his boxer shorts washes out and now they're pink.
3. His Mum says he must be in by 8.00 pm and in bed by 9.00 pm.
4. His Dad tells him not to start fights.
5. His Gran gives him kryptonite pants for Christmas.

APRIL FOOL'S DAY

Write a list of April Fool's day tricks and jokes.

Put plastic bottles outside instead of milk bottles.
Put onions in Wendy's bed.
Wrap up a stone to make a big parcel.
Stick a penny on the path.
Put salt into a pot instead of sugar.
Hide John's trousers.
Stick a cup to a saucer with superglue.

Judy Jane, 7 yrs

FOR SALE

I think the idea for selling things came when one day when someone put up a 'for sale' notice in the staff room – trying to sell off some disruptive pupil! In my class, we tried writing notices to sell off pesky younger brothers and then we moved on to selling historical artefacts such as *'Pyramid For Sale – genuine offer'*.

INVENTED INSECTS

As a child, I had a much prized copy of the *Observer's Book of Birds*. One year when I was working in a village school, I decided we would invent flies and create the *Observer's Book of Invented Flies*! We looked at several bird entries to get the gist of how to write our fly entries, drew invented flies and then wrote about them.

RED-BACKED FLY

So named because of the red stripes on its back. Flies between April and June. Eggs are seven and found underneath cars. Young found in sewers. It has scent glands on its head that give a pungent smell when alarmed.

Nancy, 9 yrs

THE LARGE-WINGED BIRD-EATING FLY

This fly is the largest specimen of the bird-eating flies. The male has a small sting at the bottom of its abdomen, which enables it to poison the bird. They lay over a thousand young but only about five survive. The female grows so heavy when pregnant that it cannot fly and that is why the male makes the nest. Their legs are so powerful that they can carry a fully grown eagle. They live in small areas of the mountains.

William, 9 yrs

CHAPTER 2
Strengthening the imagination

'Children nowadays don't have much imagination. . . they watch too much TV.' I guess that I've heard that old chestnut in staff rooms across the country. Of course, every teacher knows that the ability to imagine is important to both thinking and learning, but how do you strengthen the ability to imagine?

Imagination is the ability to think in the abstract, picturing what might happen; to create and connect items that are not actually present. A well-trained imagination can conjure up an image based on reality but may also wander playfully, creating new possibilities. Imaginative people can often understand how others might feel or envisage what might happen. It is important to remember that imagination and memory are inextricably linked – you cannot imagine what you do not know – try imagining a new colour and you'll find it is impossible!

Key imaginative skills
- To re-imagine the past so that you can 'see' it clearly.
- To hold an image in your mind so that you can 'look' carefully at it.
- To connect different items, creating something new.
- To 'see' or 'daydream' what might happen.

Imagination is essential to enjoying reading – so that the reader can enter that secondary world and live the story powerfully. It is also just as important to writing creatively.

Try playing these games to help strengthen children's ability to imagine. The games can be played as creative 'warm-ups'.

READ AND DRAW

Find a short passage from a story that either describes a person, place or event. Read it aloud and ask the children to draw what they see. They could then annotate if you re-read.

WHAT NEXT?

Read the opening from a story and ask the children to 'imagine' what might happen next – they can tell their partner or draw a mini cartoon to show what might happen.

BRING THE PICTURE ALIVE

On the interactive whiteboard, show a photo or piece of art. The children then have to imagine that they are in the photo. On mini whiteboards, ask them to list what they can see or hear, what they might feel or think if they were actually there; or use a simple talking format such as, 'I can see . . .'.

COMBINATION GAME

The teacher says an object or creature (e.g. 'tree') and the children have to see it in their imagination. Now they add in some extra detail (e.g. 'a golden tree'). Prompt them to add in what it looks like, where it is, what is is doing. Then they turn to their partner and describe what they saw.

CRAZY CHANGES

Ask the children to see an object, place or creature. Then gradually add in changes, e.g. put something on top of it, change the colour, set it alight, make it talk, make it move. Then ask them to draw or describe what they saw happening.

HOLD IT

Provide an object or image. Get the children to look carefully at it, noticing detail. Then remove it and they should try to 're-see' it in their imagination, jotting down words to describe the details. Move on from this by just giving the children a word to focus upon, e.g. cat. Tell them to look carefully at it in their imaginations. They should hold it in their minds and rapidly jot down describing words, trying hard to notice the details.

GUIDED DAYDREAM

This game helps children to develop the ability to imagine pictures. When you read to children, many fall into a sort of trance in which they seem to be staring at you with glassy eyes. They may be looking at you but actually what they are seeing inwardly is more powerful. They are creating the story in their imagination as a series of images. Writers need to develop the same ability – to see what is happening inside their minds. This is an ability that can be trained and strengthened. I call it 'doing the mad, staring thing'.

Ask the class to settle quietly and be ready to concentrate. They should stare at some small detail in the room in a fixed manner. Then you ask them to imagine a place that they know well – perhaps a room in their home. They have to try and see it in their heads. Ask them to look round the imagined room – *what is on the floor and the walls – now look out of the window – what can you see?* Gradually get them to build the picture.

Now tell them that someone is about to rush into the room and say something. *Who is it and what do they say?* Take this at a slow pace using an even tone. After a short while, ask them to tell their partner where they were, what they noticed and what happened. This can produce surprising and interesting results as well as being simply an exercise in imagining. I once tried this with a group of teachers and half a dozen of them had someone rushing in carrying a fish!

You can use guided daydreams to take them to holiday destinations, their homes, on a bus journey, into the town, into a shop. . . and to begin creating a story.

WHAT IF ...

This is a fun game and easy enough to play. Provide a starting point – a word chosen at random from a book, a photo or a piece of art. Then the children have to brainstorm as many 'what ifs' as possible.

WHAT IF . . .

What if the Mona Lisa
– began to sing like Kylie Minogue
– yawned loudly
– asked the way to the shops
– winked at me
– wrinkled her nose
– ate a double cheeseburger and fries
– took her dog for as walk
– went to live in Barnsley.

Without the ability to imagine, the world would be a duller place. Perhaps it is an ability that we ought to be developing so that children can relive their past, predict their future and enter other worlds of possibility. Einstein valued the imagination above science, for he believed that 'imagination is more important than knowledge'. Knowledge is limited – and can always be found out – but it is the imagination that will bring about new discoveries, new technologies, new thinking. Without it we are lost.

CHAPTER 3
Sentence games

Many schools have found that quick-fire daily sentence starters can have an impact on children's writing. I think that the ability to rapidly construct and vary sentences – almost without thinking about it – is one of the basic skills of writing. If children are labouring over sentence construction, this must interfere with the flow of imaginative composition. If you look at level 3 writers at the end of key stage 2, few of them can construct and vary sentences with ease, let alone adapt their sentences to create different effects.

Many children benefit from daily sentence practice. When introducing new sentence patterns remember to start orally – so they hear the pattern and then say it. This can be followed by using cards or a washing line so that they see and move the words around – kinaesthetically. Finally, they can begin to move into writing on mini whiteboards.

Keep the session speedy – writing should be automatic, not something laboured. Push the more able to develop sentences. Be ruthless on full stops! One handy tip is to say to children, 'Don't show me until you have checked'. The idea is for the children to think, write and then re-read, checking for quality and accuracy.

Link the sentence types to the type of text and to what will help children make progress. Immature writers should conquer the simple sentence. After this, ensure that the compound sentence has been accomplished. Then begin moving into the complex sentence.

Practise sentence games. Then use the same sorts of sentences in modelled and shared writing. Make sure children use the sentence types in their own writing. This is vital – try working on a sentence (or paragraph) that then has to be dropped into a longer piece of writing. Store good sentences in writing journals for future use. Collect beautifully and powerfully crafted sentences from literature and non-fiction. Display these on a board. Currently, the nation has an obsession with connectives and not enough interest in sentences and paragraphs. The games can be creative as well as a chance to display depth and wit whilst at the same time developing fluency and accuracy.

In my first term of teaching year 3s, I discovered the simple idea of sentence games. I used to write sentences on the board for children to imitate, change or improve. Recently, I read in Ted Hughes' *Letters* that he used the same sort of approach when working in a secondary school – except he used sentences by Swift. However, the children had to imitate the underlying pattern in a similar fashion.

> The way I taught grammar was to write a fairly simple but not too simple sentence from Swift on the board, and had them write five sentences copying the structure etc exactly, but with different subject and words . . . People do this very easily, and the example goes like magic through all their writing – if you do it regularly. This is the only successful method of teaching grammar I've used.

Here are some games to get you going:

PASS THE ROSE

Bring in an object or picture. The object is passed around. Each child has to say a sentence. Make lists of possibilities, e.g.:

A question – Why is the rose blushing?
A statement – The rose crumbles.
The truth – Roses usually have thorns.
A lie – That rose just winked at me.
An exclamation – Rose, run for it!
Make it talk – Would you like to smell my petals?
If I was this object I would. . . sharpen my thorns.
Yesterday this object. . . was just a shoot in the earth.
Tomorrow this object will be. . . a faded memory.
One day this object saw. . . a badger digging for worms.
This object's worst/best/saddest/strangest memory is . . . a
teacher's nose sniffing for sweet scent and being bee-stung!

LOUISA'S STORY GAME

Last term I visited Louisa's year 2 class in North Wales to see
them 'storymaking'. It was milk time; everyone was sucking
on straws or munching apple slices. Louisa hung up a large
story map and they began to tell 'The Magic Porridge Pot',
complete with actions.

The school has been learning stories and innovating on them
as a simple, pleasurable strategy for developing children's
writing. Louisa also plays a 'connectives' game. She puts the
connectives from the stories on to card. Then she begins a
simple story (*'One morning Sasha went into the forest to fetch
some firewood.'*) Next, she pauses and holds up a card. A
volunteer has to continue, using the connective (*'After a
while...she came to a castle!'*).

Some children may need prompting (*Meanwhile her gran...*).
Louisa suggests beginning with simpler connectives and
gradually adding in harder ones. It is also important to model
new ones before the children are expected to use them. There
is no reason why a similar game could not be played with
older pupils.

Once upon a time – one day – first – then – next – after that
after a while – a moment later – the next day – meanwhile
soon – at that moment – suddenly – unfortunately – unluckily
luckily – so – although – however – as soon as – now –
finally – eventually

POST-IT CONNECTIVES GAME

I first tried this game out in a school in Bristol. I was visiting a year 1 class and Rebecca had just told me the story of the three little pigs. In my journal I wrote, *Rebecca, 6 yrs, retold 3 pigs – heavy reliance on 'and then'. Played an inventing game where I tell a bit – then she had to carry on using 'next' or 'so'.*

I then wrote 'next', 'so', and 'after that' on post-its and used these for the children to point to. Jack, who was 5 years old, retold a dinosaur story just using 'and'. However, when we played the game I noted that *he was very able to play 'so' and 'next'*. His friend Joel, who was 6 years old, was *very good at the game*. I then noted that *we have to model the connectives in our speech* to help the children hear how sentences flow before they can do it for themselves.

The game is quite simple. Start a story off. After a while, pause at the end of a clause where a connective could be used. The child can then select a connective by choosing a connective card and continue the sentence or begin a new one, e.g.:

Me: The giant picked up the bag.
Child: Next he walked to his cave.
Me: The giant put the bag down and walked down to the
        river for a drink. Unfortunately, the giant fell in!
Child: So, the giant swam to the side.

MR COPYCAT

This game arose out of the post-it idea. The teacher says a sentence and the children have to listen carefully and repeat it. Vary *how* you say the sentences to make it fun – slowly, rapidly, loudly, quietly, like-a-ro-bot. Build in sentence features that will help the children make progress. The next step is for the children to innovate playfully on the pattern, e.g.:

> Teacher: Unfortunately, he fell down.
> Child a: Unfortunately, he ran away.
> Child b: Unfortunately, she went home.

This game hinges on the idea that children cannot write sentences unless they can say them. They cannot say them unless they have heard them – often in a range of contexts. Of course, for the children to be able to generate new sentences using the same underlying syntactical pattern, they have to understand what the sentences mean. This is crucial.

When playing Mr Copycat, you will find that some some children cannot repeat certain grammatical constructions. This indicates that the child is not yet at that stage of linguistic development. They therefore need to hear that construction more often. So a 'stumble' or error is of interest. It is worth starting simply and becoming increasingly complex.

Generally, the first connective children acquire is 'and' – usually within their third year. In the fourth year this broadens out. The errors they make demonstrate that the child is breaking new ground. If a child is in mid-flow with a story, it would be distracting to interrupt and probably unwise to 'correct' them. Just enjoy their story. Gentle 'recasting' of a sentence and mirroring back the standard version is helpful so that the child 'hears' the standard construction.

ADDING 'IN' AND 'ON'

The teacher says (or writes up) a short sentence such as *The dog barked*. The game is for the children to add 'in' and 'on' (remembering that you can tag on extra information at the end of the sentence or at the beginning), e.g. *although it was midnight, the frail dog, which was nearly 80 years old, barked as loudly as it could at the burglars as they stole the trout from the fishmongers.*

RANDOM WORDS

Choose a book. Ask for a number – this gives you a page to turn to. Now ask for a number – this gives you the line. Then ask for a small number – this will select a word. The children then have 15 seconds to write a sentence using the word. Then use the same process to randomly select two or three words. Can they make a sentence using those words?

If I have to work with a restless class, I just use the first word from the chosen line. Sometimes I select three or four words in this way and then the children have to work in pairs, saying a sentence at a time using the words in turn. For instance, let us say that using the dice we select the words *carrots, tired, bridge, so.*

The children then work in pairs to create four sentences in which the first sentence has to have the word 'carrots', the next had to have 'bridge' and so on. The real challenge is to create a story using this technique so that sentences actually flow, e.g.:

> Once upon a time there was a rabbit who loved eating carrots. He found that a carrot a day helped to keep him from becoming tired. One day, he dropped all his carrots into the river when he was crossing the bridge on his way home. So he jumped into the water and tried to rescue his carrots.

NOUN AND VERB GAME

Ask for a list of nouns (*engine, ruler, pencil, tree*). Then make a list of verbs (*sipped, stole, rushed, wished*). The game is to invent sentences that include a noun and a verb from the lists. This can be fun if the nouns and verbs do not match in any sensible way – you will get some quite creative solutions!

The engine sipped . . .
The ruler stole . . .
The pencil rushed . . .
The tree wished . . .

Now complete the sentences, preferably choosing unusual ideas, e.g.:

The engine sipped from a cup of silences.
The ruler stole a tongue of ideas.
The pencil rushed down the stairs and into the garden.
The tree wished it could turn over a new leaf.

Of course, you can try this game with any combination of word functions – prepositions and adjectives make an interesting challenge.

JOIN

Provide two short, simple sentences. The game is for the children to join them together so that they make one sentence. This can be done by using some form of connective. It is useful to suggest a way of joining them. For instance:

The camel ate the cake
The cake was full of dates.

You could ask the children to join the two sentences above using the word 'which':

The camel ate the cake which was full of dates.

This game is vital for children who are at level 3 and need to begin using a variety of ways (beyond 'and then') to link sentences, gaining flow in their writing. So play this often!

With older pupils and more mature writers practise joining or extending sentences using words such as *while, when, where, that, which, who.*

ANIMAL GAME

Make a list of animals. The children have to write a sentence about each one – as playful as possible. Put in certain criteria, e.g. use a simile, use two adjectives, use an adverb, use 'after', use 'when', etc.

IMPROVE

Provide a list of dull sentences that have to be made more detailed, interesting or powerful, e.g.:

The worm went.
The man got the drink.
The dog came along the road.
The woman ate the stuff.
The man looked at the stuff in the shop.

CHECK IT

Write up some sentences or a paragraph with errors for the children to check. Build in the sorts of weaknesses or mistakes that the children often make so they get used to identifying and correcting their own errors. These might include spelling and punctuation mistakes, changes in tense, slang, etc.

He runned down the lain.
She was dead frightened.
I just jumpt over the wall.
I ran home, Lucy just walked.
The play was well good.

SHORTEN

If children overwrite or write clumsily constructed sentences that are poorly formed, write these up and ask them to shorten the sentences or clarify them.

The robbers who were being chased ran down the road till they could run no more and then they decided that they would go into the cave and then they would hide in there and wait.

CHANGE THE ENDING

Provide a short sentence and ask the children to extend it by adding a chunk on at the end. Provide a list of ways, e.g. use a connective, add on an 'ing' chunk, add on a chunk using *who, which, that when, while, where, before, after*, etc.

Teddy closed the curtains.

This might become:

Teddy closed the curtains when the fireworks started.
Teddy closed the curtains while everyone was juggling.
Teddy closed the curtains before the milkman came.
Teddy closed the curtains, hoping it would keep out the sunlight.

CHANGE THE OPENING

Provide a simple sentence and ask the children to extend it by adding a chunk on at the beginning. Build up a repertoire of different ways to vary the opening to sentences, e.g. use an adverb (how), a time connective (when), an 'ing' or 'ed' chunk, one word, a simile, a prepositional phrase ('at the end of the lane – where'), an adjective, etc.

Bertie dug a deep hole.

might become:

After tea, Bertie dug a deep hole.
In the garden, Bertie dug a deep hole.
Carefully, Bertie dug a deep hole.
As fast as a ferret, Bertie dug a deep hole.
Hoping to reach Australia, Bertie dug a deep hole.

DROP IN

Provide a simple sentence and ask the children to 'drop in' something extra, e.g. adjective, adverb, a phrase or clause. Be wary of children dropping in too much! Of course, you could add to a sentence by attaching a bit to each end.

Bertie dug a hole.

might become:

Bertie dug a deep hole.
Bertie rapidly dug a hole.
Bertie, the farmer's dog, dug a hole.
Bertie, hoping he would soon see a kangaroo, dug a hole.

INNOVATING STORY SENTENCES

Write up a story sentence, then innovate. This could be done orally or on a mini whiteboard. With young children the sentences could be based on simple underlying syntactical patterns, e.g.:

Once upon a time there was a boy who lived on a farm.
Once upon a time there was a girl who lived in a forest.
Once upon a time there was a goblin who lived under a stone.

With older pupils, use this game to explore more demanding patterns and ideas. For instance, rehearse using a 'narrative hook' to engage the reader through this pattern:

Usually, Simrah enjoyed visiting his Nan.
Usually, Gaz liked going to the cinema.
Usually, Cally looked forwards to the end of the school day.

COPY

This game is an important one. Look carefully at the text type that you are teaching. Are there any particular sentence types that the children will need to be able to use in their writing? Look at the stage they are at and decide what sorts of sentences they need to be able to write in order to make progress. Model several of one type on a board, then ask the children to imitate the pattern, substituting different words. For instance, here are several 'adverb' starter sentences:

Carefully, Pie ate the doughnut.
Angrily, Jerry kicked the football.
Gently, Tina held the sandwich.

Create several more together and then use a bag of adverbs to help the children begin writing their own similar sentences using the same underlying structure. Apply in shared and independent writing. Borrow sentences from quality literature to imitate.

STORY SENTENCES

The storyteller Chris Smith suggested this game to me. Ask the children to think of a well-known story. They should then think of a dramatic or interesting part of the story and work out a sentence. Then, each child in turn says their sentence. This is an interesting game – sometimes the juxtaposition of the sentences and the images they hold creates a powerful or amusing effect.

The other way to play this game is to provide words, phrases or sentences from different stories for the children to guess.

What stories do these come from?

Down and down he climbed.
The wolf sneaked by.
Run, run as fast as you can.
The wolf climbed up onto the roof and peered down the chimney.
But tortoise just kept on going.
She only took one bite.
At night she slept in the cinders at the edge of the fire.
The lamp gleamed.
Somewhere in the darkness ahead he could hear the bull breathing.
He stared into the shield, not daring to raise his eyes.
Even the blades of grass turned to gold.

PAIRS

Ideally, for this game you need a set of small blank cards. In pairs, children write words on each side of the card. Nouns work fine. The cards are collected and handed out. Working in pairs the children use them to make up sentences or even mini stories.

An alternative to the game is for half the class to think of a noun and the other half to think of a verb. Everyone then moves round till they have found a partner from the other half of the room. Between them they have to use their noun and verb to form a sentence. This, of course, often leads to some amusing ideas. For instance, one child might choose 'bridge' and their partner may have chosen the verb 'whispering'. They might create sentences as follows:

The old bridge whispers secrets to the ducks.
Whispering between its metal teeth, the motorway bridge grinned.
The whispering bridge is visited daily by the old monks.

CHAPTER 4
Character games

Most children write stories that do not really have characters – they have two-dimensional figures who wander the landscape. The move into characterisation adds depth and engagement for the reader. Who wants to read a story about a character that they do not care about?

Stories are about characters. Character drives the plot. Probably the most important step forward is to begin thinking about what the character might be feeling or what sort of person they are. Many of these games need what I have described as 'feelings' cards. Children are given, or select, a card and then have to act out a scene, bearing in mind the 'feeling' that is written on the card. So the game might be played by one child in an angry fashion or in a bossy or shy manner. When children are inventing their own stories, they should always think about how the characters feel as this influences what they say and do. It is often the characterisation that drives events. Here is a list of feelings that can be used to make cards, one word on each side of the card.

Angry	Stupid	Friendly	Eager	Speaks without
Happy-go-lucky	Jealous	Thoughtful	Greedy	thinking
Clever	Embarrassed	Shy	Generous	Reluctant
Envious	Spiteful	Kindly	Confident	Confused
Brave	Reluctant	Quiet	Boastful	Excitable
Vain	Depressed	Foolish	Bossy	Anxious
Obsessed	Worried	Weariness	Loud	Fast-thinking
Lazy	Nit-picking	Proud	Cruel	Always wants
Lying	Selfish	Thoughtful	Clumsy	their way
Mean	Helpful	Silent	Helpless	Impatient
Lonely	Unconfident	Bitter	Hopeless	Unhealthy
Stubborn	Understanding	Afraid	Optimistic	Awkward
Courageous	Calm	Boastful	Gloomy	
Slow	Sad	Tentative	Proud	
Silly	Happy	Fearfully	Boring	

IN THE MANNER OF THE WORD

This is an old game but still worth playing every so often. Teachers tend to use it to teach adverbs. Storytellers use it to teach children how characterisation is best shown through what a character does.

A volunteer is asked to leave the room. The class decides on an adverb that shows 'how', e.g. *quietly*. The volunteer returns and asks a class member to do something 'in the manner of the word'. For instance, a volunteer might ask someone to sing 'in the manner of the word'. So the class member sings quietly. The volunteer then tries to guess the adverb. He/she keeps guessing until they have guessed correctly.

TELL ME

Chris Smith introduced me to this handy game for helping children to develop their own character. It is worth modelling how to play the game on a number of occasions as it takes some expertise to become good at it. The idea is simple enough, however. The children work in pairs. One of them begins by saying what their character is called and then leads into adding some extra information, e.g. *My character is called Skater and he lives on the edge of a huge estate.*

The partner now uses the phrase 'tell me more' to find out more information about the character. Usually this is accomplished by focusing on something that their partner has mentioned, e.g. *Tell me more about the estate.*

There are a few basic questions that must always be asked, unless the information has already come out:

Tell me how your character is feeling?
Tell me why your character is feeling like this?

These questions are important because characterisation is impossible if you do not know how the character is feeling.

It is worth having pairs demonstrate this in front of the class. There is a real skill in asking the right question to help the partner develop a character. Problems can arise if too much information is generated so the person who is developing the character has to learn when to end the game by saying, 'I have enough information now'. They then swap roles.

The children also have to learn that they do not have to use all the information generated but it can be there in the background, as David Almond told me, 'as a rucksack of possibilities'. Also, they have to think about what they have generated that might be useful and which pieces of information are not needed in their story.

THE CHANGE GAME

I am grateful to the playwright Poppy Corbett for this game. The idea is quite simple. With the children, make a fairly long list of everyday activities that you could mime, e.g. *eat a sandwich, write a story, sharpen a pencil, play a computer game, put on your shoes, brush your teeth.*

Someone is chosen to go into the middle of the room. They begin the mime (let's say, brushing teeth). Let it run for a short while and then select a volunteer who comes into the arena and asks, 'What are you doing?' the person doing the mime does not say what they are doing (brushing teeth) but says something different and unexpected, e.g. taking the dog for a walk. They then sit down and the new person has to mime whatever they have said.

Remind the children who are chosen that they have to mime what is said and in their heads think about what their reply will be when asked, 'What are you doing'? Long lists of ideas help!

CONFLICTS

Most stories are built around conflicts. Conflicts between characters are guaranteed to raise some sparks. This game can be played in many ways but the basic idea is that the children work in pairs – characters a and b. They are given a situation, e.g. a child has brought home some cooking from school. Character a is the parent who knows they should be full of praise but can see that the food is going to be disgusting. Character b is the child who is very proud and would be easily upset. Pairs then improvise.

Conflicting situations
One person has done well in a test and the other has not.
Two friends both lose a toy but they only find one.
Two friends find 50p and both need it for different reasons.
You see a friend break something of value.
You both told a lie but one now feels bad about it.
You both have an appointment at the same time by mistake
    and are both in a hurry.

PUTTING TWO DIFFERENT CHARACTERS TOGETHER

This game is similar to 'Conflicts'. However, the starting point is to give the pairs very different character types, e.g. bossy/shy. Then suggest a situation for them to improvise, e.g. you are in the playground deciding what to play.

Possible situations

A cat is stuck up a tree.

A dog is stuck down a rabbit hole.

The old lady over the road needs her shopping done.

Mum wants you to tidy the house.

The car needs cleaning.

You go into the library to do some work.

In the pet shop, you notice a sick dog.

Walking home, you hear a strange noise.

Character a	Character b
Bossy	Shy
Kind	Cruel
Sad	Happy
Lonely	Plenty of friends
Angry	Calm
Aggressive	Gentle
Mean	Generous

WHAT DOES YOUR CHARACTER REALLY WANT?

Many stories hinge around something that the main character really desires but is beyond their reach. The story is about their journey towards achieving their goal. This game is another improvisation. Set up a simple everyday scene – *in the playground, the canteen, the bus stop*. One character is already there, hanging about. Bring in a second character who really wants something. This can be written on a card and handed to the improviser. The job of the child already on the scene is to find out what the other character desires. The job of the character who enters is to keep their desire hidden but they must tell the truth!

Possible desires/wishes
To go fishing
To go to the chip shop
To learn to write
To please their parents
To swim two lengths
To play the guitar
To own a mobile phone
To have the latest computer game
To have the latest trainers
To be popular

MEETING A STRANGER

Improvise, in pairs, two strangers meeting, e.g. at a bus stop or in a queue for a concert. The game is to find out as much as you can about the other person and give as little away about yourself. You have to tell the truth and the improvisation must sound real. Alternatively, one of the characters is given a 'secret' that the other one has to discover. Another game involves one character having just seen something that is then recounted to the newcomer.

Meeting places	Possible secrets
Chip shop queue	You can talk to animals
Corner of playground	Your dad is a clown
Prison cell	Your mum is a TV star
Silent computer room in library	You have stolen from mum
Escape tunnel from prison	You have won a million
Sharing a taxi ride	You have found a ring
Waiting in the car park	You can read minds
At the launderette	Your best friend is ill
At the bus stop	Your pet dog is missing
Waiting for an audition to	Your teacher is suspected
be a hobbit	of being an alien

MONOLOGUE WARM-UP

The poet and storyteller John Rice sent me this warm-up game that is based around a monologue. Obviously, the teacher needs to model this so the children understand what is expected.

- Think of a person. . . boy or girl, man or woman.
- Give that person a job or standing in life. . . dentist, school girl, newsreader, footballer. . . anything at all.
- Where is that person's favourite place in the world?
- Is there something the person feels guilty about in his/her life?
- Who is that person closest to?
- What is your character's most annoying habit?
- What three important things does that person have in his/her wallet/purse/handbag/school bag?
- What was the last thing she/he bought on her/his credit card or with their pocket money?
- Why did he/she not tell their favourite person what it was they bought?
- Just how deep does the secret (or secrets) go?
- Will the secret ever get out? Who will let it out?

Now that you have all that information memorised, simply tell her/his story as a monologue. Engage your audience with eye contact, a sense of mystery and secrecy, and give the monologue an unexpected, dramatic climax.

DESCRIPTION GAME

This is the old 'police witness' game. You can use it to create a new character or to create an image of a character from a well-known story. One of a pair is in role as a policeman/woman. The other is witness to an event and has to describe the character – what they looked like and were doing. The policeman has to ask searching questions to build the description of the miscreant, whether it be Mr Wolf or Voldermort.

THOUGHTS IN THE HEAD

You can either use a story that the children know well or they can work from scratch and just invent. The idea is for children to create the thoughts running through a character's head. These could be drawn as a cartoon thought bubble but are more interesting as an extended monologue. Provide a scenario – children can rehearse their ideas in drawing, list making or by 'talking to the wall' or with a partner, before performing aloud.

Scenarios might include:

you are lost in an underground tunnel
you have been caught stealing food
you have just seen your best friend steal from the teacher's bag
you are told not to touch anything but can hear something moving inside a box
your mother expects you to do well in a test but you have done badly

SAY A SENTENCE TO REVEAL FEELINGS

Write up a sentence on the board. The challenge is for children to say it in different ways, using different emphasis. They could work in pairs to see which pair has discovered the largest number of variations of meaning. Alternatively, volunteers come to the front and are handed a 'feelings' card which directs them as to how to say the sentence.

Possible sentences
You don't know what I have been doing.
Is that all you can say?
So your name is Bertie.
I asked her if I could be on my own.
You have never seen anything like it.
This Saturday Billy will be staying at home.
Get out of this classroom and wait by the old clock.
Run for the plane.
That parcel is mine and does not belong to her.
Do I have to hang around here to see you or can I wait with my friends?

MIME WITH FEELING

The children can work in pairs or threes. They select a 'feelings card'. Then you provide something for them to mime. Once they have prepared, one of the team is volunteered to perform to the class who have to guess the feeling behind the mime.

Possible mimes
Brushing your teeth
Washing your hair
Typing an e-mail
Sending a text
Grooming the cat

Taking the dog for a walk
Washing up
Writing a story
Whistling or singing a song to yourself
Turning on the TV and changing channels
Blowing up balloons for a party
Packing a suitcase
Watering the pot plants
Reading the newspaper and doing a crossword
E-mailing friends

This game can be developed by asking the children to choose a 'feelings card'. They leave the room and after a few seconds have to walk in, cross to a table and sit down – all the time staying in role with the way they feel. They could say one thing to an imaginary person in the room. Everyone else has to decide how the character feels. Then use shared writing to translate this into words, making sure that the feeling is revealed by what the character does and says, 'showing' rather than 'telling'. Here are two contrasting examples showing anger and shyness.

Olav barged through the door and slammed it shut. He stormed across the room, grabbed the chair and sat down, glaring around the room. 'What are you looking at?' he snapped.

Lee slipped into the room, quietly closing the door behind her. She walked over to the table and sat down, hunching her shoulders. She stared at the floor as if there was something interesting on it beside the grey carpet. 'Hello,' she whispered, without looking up.

CHANGE WHAT IS SAID

This game explores the idea that what characters say reflects the sort of person they are or how they feel. Provide something on a board that the character says. The children then have to alter this having chosen a 'feeling' card. So, you might write up:

> 'Let's phone for the fire brigade to help get the cat down,' said Joanna.

This might be rewritten as:

> 'Look at that stupid animal stuck up there,' sneered Joanna.

One of the most interesting ways to move into developing dialogue is to use a short video clip. Turn down the sound. Ask the children to invent what is being said, picking up clues from the body language and facial expressions. They should then act out the dialogue. Then demonstrate how to move this into writing – adding in what the characters are doing, in order to avoid a stream of speech. You could add in:

- what the main character does as they are speaking:

'Hello,' said Bill, **taking a sip from his tea**.

- the listener's response:

Mel watched him as she sat down at the table.

- reveal what a character is thinking:

She wondered if he was alright.

- describe something in the background:

The kitchen door opened and Carter wandered in.

PAIRS GOSSIP ABOUT A CHARACTER

This game needs children to work in threes. One of them is the main character in a story. The other two are minor characters. The point of the game is to explore how minor characters can be used to develop a main character by revealing what they think about the character through comments they make or by providing some 'back-story'. To play the game, the minor characters gossip just out of hearing of the main character. The main character doesn't have to do anything, though they could provide a short monologue about what has happened to begin the improvisation. It helps to provide a situation.

The main character has just
- rescued a cat from drowning
- had an argument with their best friend
- come last in a test
- done better than expected in a test
- been seen crying
- been seen spending money even though poor
- had a new haircut
- arrived at school in a taxi rather than walking as usual
- been seen hanging around with new friends
- got a new mobile though penniless
- suddenly flared up into a bad temper
- started a fight
- been generous to a bully
- run away from school.

TALENTS AND OBSESSIONS

It can help to build a character if the writer gives them a particular strength or interest. Generate an ongoing list of possibilities that can be added to during the year. These can be used to provide a focus for short improvisations in which children select a 'talent' from the hat and have to talk in role about their interest, either in the hotseat or by being interviewed. Talents or interests might include:

Stamp collecting	Ballet dancing
War Hammer obsessive	*Star Trek* or *Doctor Who* fan
Computer games freak	Loves motorbikes
Computer hacker	Has mobile phone at all times
Tree climber	Loves a soap on TV
Loves ponies	Follows a football team
Crazy about music	Crazy about darts

CHARACTER NAMES

To some extent, if you find the right name for a character you can dispense with description. It is worth having an ongoing list of character names that the children build up across the year. These can be collected from phone directories, shop signs or just by being on the lookout for source material. Some place names make a good character name. On the way to Oxford, from where I live, there is a house called 'Barrington Downs'. To me that sounds like an out-of-work and rather flamboyant actor!

In this game, collect and list names. Then take a name and brainstorm ideas that the name suggests, building a mini profile of all sorts of things that we know about the character (though, in fact, it is all invented). It is best to avoid names of children in the class or school. I find nicknames work well, e.g.:

Grubber – always hungry, mucks around a lot, gets his clothes torn and dirty, doesn't really care, happy go lucky, his father works on the bins, likes watching DVDs.

The whistling kid – whistles wherever he goes, looks younger than everyone else, friendly, a bit shy, has hands in his pockets, bit of a day dreamer, lives in the flats, has no brothers or sisters, seems lonely at times.

SPOT THE CLUES

In this game, the teacher provides some sentences and the children have to spot the clues that tell the reader about the character. It is quickest if you scan a novel or short story for sentences. Here are some to get you going:

'I'm not going to do that!' snapped Dazee, stamping her foot.

Baz Butcher was a bully.

Josie slid out of the Rolls-Royce and walked towards her yacht, humming a tune to herself.

Boysie wondered whether he would make the first team.

She was small, slim and frail looking, rather like a red-haired elf.

Mr Muckletooth collapsed on to the front seat, wiped a tear from his eye and wondered what to do next.

Mrs Snortwart felt annoyed by her daughter's success.

CHARACTER DEVELOPMENT

Most stories are about people and what happens to them, and how this changes them. In this sense, stories are about transformations. When developing a story, it can help to decide on how the character is at the beginning and therefore what they are likely to be like at the end. For instance, if you have a lonely character at the start of the story, the likelihood is that a friendship will have developed by the end. There are probably many ways of exploring this idea. Add to the grid below by thinking of transformations in common fairy tales. These tend to reflect the prime movements and transformations.

In this game, the children write an opening and ending line from a story that shows the two different states, e.g.:

Opening showing loneliness – Coral stood on her own while everyone else rushed around the playground.

Ending showing a friendship found – Coral grinned at Caitlin as they ran out of school.

Opening	Ending
Rags	Riches
Lonely	Friendship
Sad	Happy
Angry	Calm
Cruel	Kind
Illness	Health
Imprisoned	Freedom
Badly treated	Looked after
Liar	Truthful
Violent	Gentle
Empty	Full
Afraid	Brave
Idle	Hard-working
Injustice	Justice
Empty	Full
Foolish	Wisdom
Selfish and mean	Generous
Evil	Good

STORIES BASED ON CHARACTERS

Here is a list of simple ideas for stories based around typical characters. Many of them are ideas taken from well-known traditional tales. The children can invent orally their own stories to tell. This can be done in pairs, with a simple story map. Or they plan and sketch on their own before working as a pair, using their partner as a response partner. They will need to have a chance to retell their tale at least three times in order to begin to rehearse and gain fluency.

Tell a story in which:

- A girl or boy is being held captive by a bad person but manages to escape in the end.
- A kind character is always helping animals. He or she is put into a prison but manages to escape with the help of the animals.
- A young person leaves their kind mother and sets out into the world, travels and has adventures, but eventually returns to find the mother has disappeared.
- A giant moves into the land. Everyone is afraid of the giant except for a small child who discovers that it is lonely.
- Three young people are sent out into the world to seek their fortune by an ageing parent. They return at the end.
- Elves have been living nearby but their land is about to be destroyed. They are helped by a child.
- Three young people are sent out into the world to find a specific item to please an aged parent.
- A child finds a gateway or door into a fairy world. They warn the child not to touch something but the child is tempted. They chase the child away.
- The king or queen is dying and a young person has to seek a cure in time.
- A child is left alone, following a great disaster. The child has to journey to escape and three events happen on the journey, each worse than the previous. In the end there is a joyful and unexpected reunion.

- Three sisters/brothers have different characteristics: bossiness; poor at listening; and kind. They travel somewhere one by one.
- A young person finds a miniature dragon and keeps it as a secret but bad people want to steal the dragon for their own ends, e.g. put it in a zoo.
- A princess or prince is given a special object to guard (shoe, ball, crown, goblet, cloak, seeds, mirror, sack, chest, ring) but loses it or has it stolen. How is it regained?
- Three brothers (or sisters) attempt to rescue the fourth who has been stolen. The third is physically weak but kind and clever. The weak one wins through.

CHAPTER 5
Games to develop settings

IN THE CITY OF ROME

We used to play this old game in the back of the car on long journeys. It is ideal for building descriptions of settings. It develops the ability to visualise a setting. Think of a place and identify one thing that you can see (a park bench). Then say, *In the city of Rome is a park bench.*

The next person has to repeat what you have said and add in something else, e.g. *In the city of Rome is a park bench and under the bench is a sleeping dog.* This game seems to me central to the whole business of helping the children develop the ability to create settings. They should just build the setting – not have anything happening.

Pass the line on, with each child adding something else they can see or hear. Try playing the game in groups and pairs till the children can visualise and describe a scene in their own mind. The game is not so much a memory test but just develops the ability to see and create a scene. Once the description has become too long to recall, they can start again, perhaps choosing a different setting.

For instance, instead of 'In the city of Rome', play the game using the setting in their story, e.g. 'In the haunted house'. They can add in descriptive details and then, at a key moment, the game changes. They shift to saying 'at that moment', and have something happen. This can be followed by using 'after that'. In this way the story begins to take shape.

Show children how to sketch the scene that has been created and annotate, adding in similes. Then practise turning the scenes into mini paragraphs.

Try using the game to create a setting based on places that the children know well so that they get used to drawing on their own experiences. Explain how settings can be made more interesting by introducing one element that is out of place or unexpected – something that they can see or hear, perhaps.

Try varying the preposition. For instance, you could have children working in pairs and use, alternatively, 'inside' and 'outside'. They think of a place such as a palace and then proceed thus:

a. Inside there is a log fire blazing.
b. Outside the snow has covered the land.
c. Inside a prince paces up and down.
d. Outside the prince's horse shivers.

Play variations of this game many times to help children be able to play it inside their own minds.

YOU CAN SEE...

I got this idea from the poet James Carter who had been experimenting with it in writing workshops. Since then I have developed it further. The basic idea is as the previous game. The children work in pairs and one of them has to describe their setting for their partner using the words, 'You can see . . .'. They also describe what can be heard, smelt or the feel of something significant.

When playing this game, at first the setting is not very clear in your mind but as you add in more detail, more appears. It helps if you train the children to visualise the scene and to look around it rather like a camera scanning a view.

I have since developed this further into a simple drama game that works well if the children are used to playing variations of 'in the city of Rome'. Children can work in small groups or pairs. Of course, the game needs modelling many times.

The idea is that one of the pair is in role as a character from a story and has to describe the place they are in to their partner. It can help to give them a starter. For instance, if Bilbo Baggins has just walked into an Elf's den, he might begin:

> I can see the walls lined with green leaves. There is a small case of golden wands on the floor. By the door hangs an elf's cloak of silver. . .

It helps if you make a list with the children of various prepositions. The secret to playing the game is for the speaker to try to visualise the setting in their mind.

Above	In the corner	Under the
On top of	By the	Beneath
Beside	On the ceiling	Inside
Below	From the ceiling	Outside
Underneath	On the floor	Along the

SETTINGS TO CREATE ATMOSPHERE

Scan books and collect descriptions of settings. Compile a wall display and label them. What sort of atmosphere do they create? Why has the author paused to describe the setting? List cosy settings (home, school, park) and scary settings (alleyway, forest, empty house).

Look carefully at scary settings to see how the author actually makes a setting sound frightening. This could be by using a sound effect (footsteps, a scratch, a low moan, a scream) or a glimpse of something out of place (a hand, feet, a red eye). Notice how scary settings often involve placing the main character in a lonely, dark place and then have something unexpected or out of the ordinary happen.

Coral tiptoed into the dusty room. Her footsteps echoed but she carried on. She could just see the old machines towering above her, moonlight from the skylight covering them in a silvery sheen. The shadows seemed darker than ever. At that moment, she heard a door open and felt a rush of cold air. Somebody or something was moving towards her. She could see its vague outline . . .

MIMING A SETTING

To play this game it helps to begin with a long list of possible settings. A volunteer or pair identifies a setting, comes out and mimes entering the setting and doing something. The rest of the class have to guess the setting. It helps if they rehearse their mime in pairs, discussing ideas:

By the roundabout in the park
By the ice cream van
In the cinema
In the queue in Tesco's
Walking home
Locked in your bedroom
Under the stairs at home
In a stable with a horse
On the Moon
In a box afloat on the sea

MIXED SETTINGS

This is an amusing game to play, which Teddy Corbett suggested to me. Use the list below (and extend it with more ideas from the children). The idea is to randomly select an item from each list. Rehearse a mime or improvisation in pairs and then pairs or individuals come into the centre to perform their mime. Everyone else has to guess the combination. For instance, you might be in a chip shop in the middle of a desert.

Everyday place	Position	More unusual setting
Chip shop	in	the desert
Bus stop		a cave
Launderette	near	dark forest
Classroom	by	a lift
Playground		police station cells
Kitchen	beside	fishing boat on stormy sea
Swings in the park	close to	leaking petrol pumps
Burger King		a pet shop by a gorilla
Car park	at	New York – airport lounge

IMAGES

Use an image of a setting on the IWB. This could be simply achieved by googling images for cities, parks, forests, streets and so forth. Alternatively, a digital camera can be used by children to develop images of the school and the surroundings that could be used for a school-based adventure. There are many quick-fire games that could be played. For instance, in one minute, jot down descriptive sentences. What can you see and hear?

However, it might be just as inviting to use the image to create some possibilities for creating a narrative. Use these sorts of questions to generate some creative thinking:

• One of these characters has a secret. Which one and what is the secret?
• Something is hidden here. Where and what?
• One of these characters is about to get a mobile phone call. Who from and what is about to be said?

- Something has been lost here. What is it, who lost it and what will happen if they do not find it.
- Someone here is about to drop something valuable. Who, what and what will happen as a result?
- One character here has an unusual hobby. Who is it and what is their interest?
- One person here had just told a terrible lie. Who is it, what was the lie they told and to whom, and what will happen as a result?
- Something is buried here that is important. What is it, where is it and who will find it?

IMAGINATIVE IMAGES

Over the years I have built up a collection of postcards for writing. Soppy seaside sunsets don't work well, but postcards of paintings (e.g. Dali, Magritte) or photographs provide an endless source of material. Images can be used for descriptive writing. Alternatively, an image can be used to generate a story. Ask the children to pretend that the picture is the front cover of a book. What might the story be called? What sort of story might it be? What might happen? Who are the main characters? Another approach is to pretend that the picture they have selected comes from a story book and is illustrating a scene in a story. They can then retell or write that section of the story.

One ideal use for the IWB is to hold a bank of photos, paintings and film clips of people and places. For instance, show a short clip of two characters. The children search for clues to deduce how the characters feel, noticing what they say and do. Follow this by reading a passage of dialogue and seek the same sorts of evidence; or turn down the volume and invent the dialogue. Translate the dialogue into writing and see how you have to add in extra detail so the reader can picture who is speaking and what is happening. Use the same idea to develop settings. Imagine that you are in the setting. What can you see, hear and feel? Annotate and use images and descriptive language to build the setting.

Treat films like the daily class reader. Michael Morpurgo's *When the Whales Came* or Diana Wynne Jones's *Howl's Moving Castle* can be used to lead into drama, interpretation, comparison with the novel or as a stimulus for writing. To develop settings, pause at key moments to discuss how the setting changes to create moods. Turn a still image from a film into a short description.

THE GREEN CHILDREN

This is my version of the story of 'The Green Children'. I sometimes use it to lead into a game to help children create imaginary worlds and settings. Read or tell the story first.

It was harvest time.

We were down by the wolf-pits playing
when we first saw them.

Stumbling out of the cave,
Blinking at the daylight,
Babbling strange sounds.

They stood stock still, shock still –
And so did we.

For they were green –
Green as the leaves on the trees,
Green as the grass on the wayside,
Green as corn in the spring-time.

We took them home and offered them bread –
But all that they would eat were beans from the pod.

But the boy grew pale and took to his bed
And seven months on they found him dead.

But the girl married Lenna and told us their tale –
They came from St Martin's land,
A sunless land
Where the bright country can be seen
Across the great river.

Brother and sister, they had followed their flock into a cavern
Where they had followed the sound of bells
That led them into our bright world.

Now she's grown older and her skin is like ours,
But once in a while she wiles away the hours,
Back in the past, lost in another world.

This all happened in the reign of King Stephen,
A cart horse's ride from Bury St Edmunds.
So says I, Ralph of Coggeshall.

I use this story to offer a chance to role play what the Green Children said when they described their own land. The Green Children could be interviewed or hot seated. You could ask them to create a monologue to explain to the village folk what their land looked like. Villagers could ask them questions to help the children develop their ideas. It helps to rehearse in pairs or threes.

This leads quite nicely into the idea of stories that have a 'portal' through which characters travel from one place to another. This idea is used in many stories – many children will have seen the portal on the television programme *Stargate*. They will also know the story of *The Lion, the Witch and the Wardrobe*. List possible portals and then mime moving through a portal and travelling from our real world into another place. This could be enhanced by reading from the Narnia book. In pairs, children develop an oral description of the place they travel into.

TELLING STORIES BASED ON KEY SETTINGS

There are certain settings that act as powerful motifs in stories. For instance, travellers who meet a mountain range have reached a metaphorical barrier. However, a mountain to climb is a barrier that will be overcome when the main character reaches the peak.

It is worth using settings cards for children to choose a key landscape. Discuss what might happen there and how it will influence the story. Key settings that influence stories are:

Mountains	Lake	Stream
Hills	Pool	Palace
Hillside	Pond	Tower
Hedge	Oceans	Maze
Fence	Sea	Castle
Wall	Rivers	Forests
Dark woods	Swamp	Gates
Thicket	Doors	Bridges
Kitchen	Cosy bedroom	Workshop
Great hall	Library	Tower

THE SEASONS GAME

Creating a setting is not just about the place – if you are outside, it is also about the time of the day, the weather and the season. Try an interview game in which one person is in the hot seat. This person has thought about a setting. The job of the rest of the class or group is to ask questions to help develop the setting. It can help if you say that there needs to be ten specific things in the setting for the class to discover. It is interesting if one of these is unexpected or out of place. It helps if the person in the hot seat must answer truthfully.

MEMORY SEARCH

Train children to use their own memories of places that they know well. These make ideal settings for stories because they are well known, so when describing the setting the children can draw on real detail. Use a guided daydream to help the children picture a favourite place such as a holiday destination, their bedroom at home, a den or secret place that no adults know about. From bus shelters to garden sheds, secret places make useful starting points for stories.

- Who might break in and why?
- Would they destroy the den?
- Who might live in such a place?
- What do you keep there?
- How do you stop others finding your secret place?
- What can you see from there?
- You have found someone or a creature and hide them in a secret place – but someone finds them.
- Make a pretend mobile phone call to explain to a friend what is happening.

HOLIDAY PROGRAMME

In pairs, develop an introduction to a place on a pretend holiday programme. The children are in role as presenters and have to introduce the viewers to a setting, describing where they are and what it is like in order to persuade the viewers to take a holiday there. They only have one minute to sell the place. This could be a building, in which case the children can describe some of the rooms.

CHAPTER 6
Storymaking games

Now we come to the heart of this book. What sort of games can we play in the classroom to help children develop confidence and fluency in telling whole stories? There are a few key principles that lie behind these games and it might be worth me spelling these thoughts out right now before we get stuck in.

Storytelling is natural to human beings. Many of us have spent our lives telling stories about what has happened to us and what might happen next. We are storytelling machines whether we like it or not. It is our natural disposition. How can a teacher tap into this natural disposition? It might be worth saying that 'fear' is the enemy of creativity. It is the fear of somehow 'getting it wrong' that usually halts children – or any of us – in their tracks.

So when working on storytelling, it is worth being endlessly positive. We clap children and always stress what worked well, what we liked, what was interesting. In the current climate of league tables and tests such an idea might seem alien – can we really help children make progress without pointing out where they are going wrong? If we praise and highlight strengths and achievements, these are likely to be repeated by that child but also emulated by their classmates. In this way, we can learn from each other what works and gradually develop together. A positive approach builds a 'can do' attitude and also encourages children to work hard – it motivates! There can be little learning without motivation. If there is a point to be made, the teacher could always demonstrate a weakness themselves for the class to identify and provide advice on how a telling could be improved.

One important part of any creative game is that it is alright if you cannot think of anything to say – mistakes can be just as interesting as 'getting it right'.

Some of these games rely on the children knowing a bank of traditional tales – many of the games are aimed at helping children learn such stories. Many games look at retelling these tales by embellishing or altering in a playful manner. Developing confidence in storytelling by using known tales means that the teller does not have to worry about the basic plot and can concentrate on manipulating the words and sentences, creating within the boundaries of a known framework or blueprint. Here is a basic list of key stories for you to add to:

The Little Red Hen	Jack and the Beanstalk
The Gingerbread Man	Cinderella
The Billy Goats Gruff	The Three Wishes
The Three Little Pigs	Rumplestiltskin
The Three Bears	Baba Yaga
Hansel and Gretel	Red Riding Hood
Snow White	Aesop's Fables, e.g. The Hare
Theseus and the Minotaur	and the Tortoise
King Midas	Icarus

You may want to use some of these games for the children just to 'have a go' as a limbering-up session. On the other hand, the game may develop into something more substantial. If children are developing a told story they do need time to rehearse and develop their telling. This is best done in pairs, with time to work on their story, retelling a number of times to develop fluency and confidence.

TELLING A STORY WORD BY WORD

This is a key game in storymaking. It involves sitting in a story circle and creating, or retelling, a story word by word round the circle. So the first person might say 'once' and then the next person has to say the next word in the sentence, e.g. 'there' and so on:

once. . . there. . . was. . . a. . . snake. . . that. . . lived. . . in . . .

Begin by modelling the idea with several pupils. You can try it with the whole class so that they get the idea but this can be tedious for the 30th pupil!

Challenge groups, threes or pairs to keep the story going. The skill is to maintain the story and not kill it off with a joke or something silly to raise a laugh – though this can be occasional fun! Can a group develop a simple plot and retell it for the class by standing in a line?

Use the game to retell a story that they have been told and are trying to learn; or use it to innovate or invent a totally new story.

This story game challenges the preconceived story that is developing in the mind. This can be at text or sentence level. It forces creative use of language. Let the children have fun sessions as well more serious attempts to develop something that might actually work as a story. Try using a fluent writer as scribe in each group.

You can lob in extra challenges such as verbalising and signing punctuation marks, using connectives or other language features. Only try this when the children become experienced at the basic game.

STORY ROUND THE CIRCLE

In essence this is the same game as the one above, except the children say a sentence at a time rather than a word. At first this is usually playful and children enjoy making the story take new and unexpected twists and turns. However, the game can be played to help children learn a story and retell it. It can be used to retell and innovate as well as generate a totally new story. Try using a fluent writer as scribe in each group. Try adding in extra challenges by using character or setting or problem cards. Try pausing the class in mid flow and lobbing in an extra challenge – this could be at text level (*your main character's pathway is blocked*) or linguistic (*you must start the next sentence with 'unfortunately'*).

It is worth having pairs, threes or small groups out front to perform the game with others watching. This provides a chance to consider what spoils or helps a story as it develops co-operatively. In this way guidelines can be drawn up.

Try using different ways into a story that generate interest and excitement:

- One member from each group comes to the front and chooses an object from a story box or bag. This has to be incorporated into the story and is also passed round the circle as the tale develops.
- Give each member of the group a key word that they have to use at some point. For instance, these might be settings, characters or problem words:

Settings	Characters	Problems	Positive words
Woolworths	Father Christmas	Storm	A helper arrives
Disco	Robber	Thunder	A magic wish
Garden shed	Teacher	Snow	Dream is true
Hospital waiting	Princess	Hurricane	Unicorn appears
room	Queen	Tornado	A magic ring
Garage	Singer	Earthquake	found
Corner shop	Policeman	Robbery	Phone rings
Dentist	Doctor	Lost	Map is found
Beach	Explorer	Kidnapped	Treasure is found
Cross Channel	Inventor	Anger	Flying horse
Ferry			appears
Castle			Friends arrive

- It might be helpful if one member of the group is given a card with a positive idea or word written upon it, which can be played when things are going from bad to worse, e.g. a helper arrives; a magic wish is granted; a dream comes true.

The skill of this game is to end up with something that really does flow well as a story. It is actually easier to throw in a 'googly' rather than follow the trail of a story, crafting the tale as it develops.

DRAW IT!

When children are trying to learn a story with a view to retelling it and developing it into their own version, drawing a storymap or storyboard is essential. It helps the children capture the essence of the plot as well as beginning the process of visualising the tale and recalling its underlying pattern. Storymapping has been shown to be an essential aspect of storymaking. With younger children, the teacher draws a class map and then the children copy this. Older children listen to a story and after several 'tellings' can draw the map. This is then used for their 'retellings' in pairs. You can use:

- Storymap, mountain or graph.
- Cartoon, storyboard.
- Flow chart, boxes or paragraph planner.

Younger children may draw or paint whole scenes and these can be displayed on a class wall or in a Big Book to show the sequence of events.

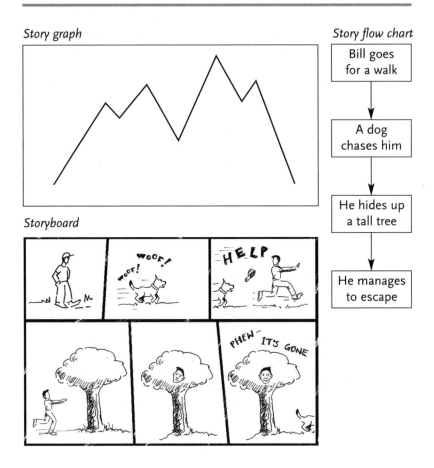

Story graph

Storyboard

Story flow chart

Bill goes for a walk

↓

A dog chases him

↓

He hides up a tall tree

↓

He manages to escape

WALK THE STORY STEPS

Many children find this activity very handy. If they are trying to learn a story and develop their own retelling, they can work with a partner and just run through the key events, taking a step at a time. There is something about the physicality of stepping out events that seems to help children to remember them. Try this as a whole class with a simple story so that everyone knows what to do. In some schools the teachers have created a long storymap by joining large pieces of paper together. This is set down in the hall and then the children walk beside the map, looking at the images and telling the story.

My guess is that mapping and stepping are activities that could be used for many forms of learning, e.g. learning scientific concepts.

EXCUSES

Excuses are always needed. When I was a child I was endlessly late and homework was a mystery to me! Make a list of excuses – the more exaggerated the better. Here are some year 4s in full flight:

> This morning I was late for school because there was a knock on my door and I opened it to find that the local farmer had just dumped a lorry load of horse manure on my doorstep. I had to dig myself a route to the front gate.

> This morning my head teacher was late for school because his Lotus Elan was jammed at the lights when star performers from Sir Serendipity's Travelling Flea Circus had escaped. They had to be hunted down and recaptured before the traffic could move.

TELL THE STORY BEHIND THE CLICHÉD SIMILE

Look at the list common similes below and ask the children to explain to their partner the story behind the simile. Try inventing new similes and listing them. Collect the best from scanning poems and novels. Make class lists. Discuss why a simile works – is it just a visual similarity? Create a simile alphabet in pairs or small groups within a few minutes.

As brave as a lion
As busy as a cat on a hot tin
  roof
As cunning as a fox
As deaf as a post
As dry as dust
As happy as Larry
As happy as a rat with a gold
  tooth
As hungry as a bear
As hungry as a wolf
As innocent as a lamb
As mad as a hatter
As wise as Solomon

As patient as Job
As poor as a church mouse
As proud as a peacock
As scarce as hen's teeth
As silly as a goose
As slippery as an eel
As slow as a tortoise
As sly as a fox
As stubborn as a mule
As thin as a toothpick
As timid as a rabbit
As tricky as a box of monkeys
As welcome as a skunk at a
  lawn party

THE STORY WORD WAITER

The poet Brian Moses once wrote a poem along this line that involved a 'word waiter' who could serve up only a certain number of words. This can be used for short-burst writing, haiku, letters or news items. The randomness of the selection adds a challenging edge that often forces creativity beyond the predictable. The word waiter might serve up a character, place and dilemma for storytelling. Here are some possible starters – but ask the children and add many more ingredients.

Character	Place	Dilemma
Woodcutter	Hairdressers	Gets lost
Farmer	Station	Is chased
Princess	Bus stop	Steals something
Adventurer	Cinema	Is trapped
Heroine	Castle kitchen	Sees a fight
Billy	Old bridge	Finds a cave
Jo	Chip shop	Loses money
Teacher	Wooden tower	Finds an alien

STORY TENNIS

This game is quite fun. It is a development of the 'telling a story word by word' game. The children work in teams and sit facing each other. The story is developed word for word with each child taking turn and the words flying backwards and forwards. If anyone stops or has to pass they are out. You will need someone who keeps score and acts as tennis umpire!

TELLING YOUR STORY TO A TREE

When children are developing their own story or retelling orally, they will need to have drawn a storymap or storyboard. Holding this, they can then find a tree in the playground, a mark on the wall or a teacher's car and enter a private world. Blocking everything else, they should rehearse their tale, reworking sentences until they gain fluency and confidence. Children love the slightly whacky approach to this idea.

HEADLINES

Choose several headlines from the newspapers. Swap pieces over to create a new headline. Children work in pairs to tell the news story behind the headline. I have just tried this, using today's papers:

Woman admits putting rat poison in a spare room by the sea
Athletes facing tests on their hair to plunge 500,000 into the dark!!

Or, extract several sentences from different stories, cut in half and join to create a new sentence. Adjust the syntax and use as a starting point for children to tell the story.

STOLEN STORY FRAGMENTS

This is an interesting challenge. Ask the children to select fragments from different stories by looking in books. They should select phrases, short sentences or even words. These can be put into a story bag drawn on the board. Then tell a story weaving in as many of the fragments as possible.

An alternative game is to make a list of stories that everyone knows. Then brainstorm words that the children can think of that somehow encapsulate or represent the story. The challenge is to select say five of these words and weave a story using the ideas or words themselves.

STORY SUMS

Provide a string of words for the children to use as a basis for a told story set out like a sum. Begin with something that is rather obvious. For instance:

Dog + cat + chase + tree + bucket of water + dog + run away

When they become good at turning these story sums into little tales, move into selecting words more randomly to challenge creativity. Here is a random story starter:

Kevin + ticket + bus + broken mobile = ?

It helps if you give a character at the start.

OPENINGS AND ENDINGS

Collect opening and ending sentences from well-known stories or books. Put these on a list, muddling them up. The first game to play would be to see if the children can match up the right opening and ending. They could then select an opening that appeals and invent a new story. Research shows that when children are provided with an ending, their writing improves because the narrative moves towards a specific end-point rather than rambling. So ask children to choose an ending they then use to create a new story. Alternatively, all vote for a favourite opening and ending, then everyone has 30 minutes quiet writing to see what different stories can be developed.

Collect opening sentences that have a problem in the first line. Invent similar sentences and use these as a basis for creating stories, e.g.:

> The giant roared as it approached the village.
> The tornado spun.
> The old bridge collapsed.
> Gary was locked in the castle and there was no way out.
> The wolf stared at Joanna.

Provide opening paragraphs to act as story triggers, e.g.:

> His name was Toy Jubilee and he was the largest person that I had ever met. My grandfather had warned me not to hang around with Toy but that made it even more tempting. 'They think they're better than us,' he said, smiling benignly. But I knew better.

Collect and display endings – or write them into writing journals. Rehearse making up storymaps and ideas to lead towards a specific ending.

GETTING YOUR HOOKS INTO A STORY

Two people had secrets up on the roof of Riverside School. Curiosity provides a tempting start to Bernard Ashley's *Break in the Sun*. Who are they – why are they on the roof – and what are their secrets? Opening a story with a 'hook' arrests the reader. Try sifting through stories to find different types for future use and categorise them.

Many stories begin with a dangerous object: *Where's Papa going with that axe?* (*Charlotte's Web*). Other stories start off with the main character introducing tension by denial: *I don't scare easily* (*The Phantom Thief* – Pete Johnson). These hooks foretell that the main character will be put into a frightening situation.

How Hedley Hopkins Did a Dare (Paul Jennings) begins by introducing a setting with an ominous element: *They say there is something awful in the sand dunes.* Again, we know that the main character will face whatever lurks in the dunes. Another type of 'hook' places the main character directly in danger: *I disappeared on the night before my twelfth birthday* (*Kensuke's Kingdom* – Michael Morpurgo). Collect and list examples in the children's writing journals. Use these as a basis for creating their own hooks (*Sanjay didn't believe in ghosts*).

DILEMMAS

Collect a long list of all the sorts of things that 'go wrong' in a story. Use these to invent new stories. A simple game is for a pair to tell a quest story in which a character is travelling from one place to another, which has to include three problems. Let the children select from the list. Problems may include:

You get lost	No-one will help
Something of value is stolen	A wish goes wrong
There is an argument	A barrier stops you
There is a famine	Someone is trapped
Bullies chase you	You get hurt
There is an accident	A wish goes wrong
A lie is told	An invention fails
Someone is kidnapped	A storm destroys a bridge
Something of value is lost	A snake appears
A monster attacks	Wolves attack

UNFORTUNATELY...

This is a very common game that we used to play as children. Work in pairs. One person starts the game by giving a short story beginning, e.g. *Once upon a time there was a king who liked eating doughnuts.* The partner now responds saying 'unfortunately', e.g. *Unfortunately, there were no doughnuts left.* The partner now comes back with 'luckily', e.g. *Luckily, the baker had just made some.* They keep on going until one can manage no more!

We have experimented with this game by trying out other connectives such as, 'after that', e.g. *After that the king ate some fresh ones from the baker. After that, the baker had to bake some more.*

We then tried using 'after that' plus 'however', e.g.:

After that the baker had to bake some more.
However, the oven would not work.
After that the baker had to go to use his friend's oven.
However, lightning struck and that oven was ruined . . .

Experiment with different combinations to find ones that flow and are fun to use. Linguistically, it is a helpful game because children are using a variety of somewhat unusual structures – adverb starters and connective starters.

PASS THE STORY ON

Hold a story assembly. Whisper a short tale into one child's ear. This child has to pass the story on by whispering it to someone else. In this way everyone hears and passes the story on. Hold another assembly at the end of the day. Try and find the last person to hear the take. Has it changed? You could use this one:

> **ENDLESS TALE**
>
> It was a dark and stormy night,
> And the land was not in sight,
> When up stood the Captain who said,
> 'Let's have a tale to warm our hearts
> and soothe our fear so far from home.'
> So up stood the First Mate who said,
> 'It was a dark and stormy night,
> and the land was not in sight',
> when up stood the Captain who said,
> 'Let's have a tale to warm our hearts . . .'

FICTIONALISING ANECDOTES

Most writers use incidents from their own life. They constantly draw on places, people and events, dressing them up or adapting them. Betsy Byars called these mini incidents 'scraps'. Anne Fine reckons that you get ideas from everywhere.

> You learn to recognise what sort of thing can make a story or fit in a book. You find yourself thinking, 'I can use that', and making a note on a piece of paper. I even have a file of scrappy messages to myself, some now totally incomprehensible even to me, called 'Things to use Later'. (from *An Interview with Anne Fine* (Mammoth Egmont (1999))

Of course, the one thing that all children have is their own life as a resource for narrative writing. However, many of the stories that they attempt are so distant from their experience that they get used to inventing everything that happens. This often makes the story sound hollow and unreal.

Anecdotes are an excellent starting point for writing. Draw three columns on the board – *places, people, events*. Make a note of key places – where you were brought up, secret places, holiday places, places that you vividly remember, scary places. . . Then list unusual people – odd relatives or neighbours, frightening or funny people. Finally, make a list of events – moving home, new school, starting school, scary or funny things, getting lost, getting into trouble. . .

Sad times	Running away
A friend moving away	Breaking something
Strange places	Stealing
A frightening person	Tricks
My worst memory	April fool
Grandad/ma	Moving school/house
Frightening events	Making new friends
A row	Breaking friends
A funny thing that happened	My best place
Getting lost	My best holiday
Getting hurt	Getting caught out
Being frightened	Crazes
	Losing something precious

Now tell some anecdotes arising from the list. They do not have to be very dramatic – something simple like being sent to the corner shop and losing the money will do. Once you have told a few anecdotes, get the children in pairs telling and retelling their own. Show them how to change the anecdote into a story by changing from first to third person, using a different name. For instance, I sometimes tell the children about a party that I went to as a child:

It was the first birthday party that I had ever been to and I was feeling a little bit nervous but also excited. Everything went well until we had to play a game that involved putting your hand into a bag and feeling an object. You had to guess what was in there. So I stuck my hand in the bag and felt something slippery and round. I thought that it was an eyeball so I screamed and screamed. But it turned out to be a grape that someone had peeled!

Now to turn this into a short story, begin by thinking of a name for the main character:

> It was the first birthday party that Gary had ever been to and he was feeling a little bit nervous. . . .

To give the telling more depth, show the children how to plan it on to a five-part story mountain:

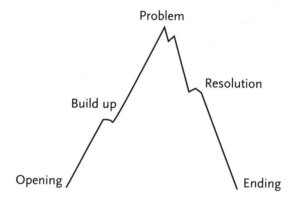

Opening – *Gary goes to the party*
Build up – *the game begins*
Problem – *he touches the eyeball*
Resolution – *it turns out to be a grape*
Ending – *he feels foolish*

Now retell Gary's story and then write it up, using the five-part structure to create paragraphs. Real details can be added in or invented:

> It was the first birthday party that Gary had ever been to and he was feeling a little bit nervous but also excited. He arrived at exactly eight o'clock and soon realised that most of the children were from his class.
>
> After tea, Mrs Jenkins took them into the sitting room to play games. They began with 'musical chairs' and 'dead donkeys'.

Then Mrs Jenkins brought out a large bag. They all took it in turn to put their hand into the bag to see if they could guess what was inside. Mrs Jenkins called it a 'feely bag'.

Gary didn't like the idea of sticking his hand into the bag. He waited quietly, hoping Mrs Jenkins wouldn't notice him. But it didn't work. 'Now then young man, pop your hand in and have good feel around.' Gary's hand seemed to have a life of its own. He didn't want to put it into the bag. But in it went! At first, he felt nothing. Then he touched something round like a marble but it was slippery. He knew what it was. It was an eyeball!

Gary's scream broke the silence and within a second everyone else was screaming too! It took quite a while to settle him down after that, but in the end, Mrs Jenkins opened the bag and showed Gary what he had touched. It wasn't an eyeball; it was a peeled grape! Everyone laughed and Gary felt a little bit foolish.

Later on, Gary's mum came to fetch him home. 'Say thank you for having me,' she reminded him, as they left. It was dark outside. As they walked down the street, she dug her hand into her coat pocket and brought out a small bag. 'Here, have a toffee, love,' she said. Gary stared at the bag. Inside he could hear the sweet papers rustling. Gary loved toffees – but for the first time in his life, he said no!

THE STORY JIGSAW

Cut up a story, such as a fairly short traditional tale, into five sections. Put the children into groups of five. Each group then prepares their section for telling. They should know how to do this – draw a map, tell round the circle, work in pairs or threes. After an allotted time, children then form new groups so each group has one representative from the original groups – therefore, the whole story. They sit in a circle and tell the tale in order, piece by piece.

STORY SOUP

I have used this idea many times as a workshop. On a board make a list of traditional tales. Then list good/bad characters, animals, objects, settings and dilemmas from traditional tales. The more the children can remember, the better. The children then have to choose from each section and in this way create their own little story recipe to invent a new story. They can, of course, steal a story idea and recast it. Here are some simple ingredients that might be stirred into a story soup:

Beginnings
– There once was a . . . who had to . . .
– Once upon a time there was a . . . who wanted . . .
– There once lived . . . who decided to . . .

Endings
– and so the giant went back to the forest and was never seen again.
– and so the two children threw the key into the river and began to make their way home.

Themes
– magical wishes; wanting something; having to make a journey to find something or someone; making a journey to rescue or save someone or something; something of value is lost or trapped; a character begins in great poverty but ends with riches; a lonely character finds friendship; a mean or cruel character is overcome.

Settings
– dark cave; magical fountain or garden; mysterious doors; a gateway into another world; beautiful palace; paths and roads to follow; sunlit stream; deep cavern; underground tunnel; treehouse; cloud city; mountains or hills to cross; magical pools; stormy seas; dark forests; lonely tower; villages and towns; market place; wooden shack.

Characters

- king or queen; prince or princess; mother; father;
  grandparent; farmer; poor old person; cruel tyrant;
  ferryman; wise woman; miller; brothers and sisters; person
  who is sad and has never laughed; enchanter; servant;
  trickster; hero or heroine; fool; friendly cook; ogre or giant;
  troll; woodcutter; gnomes; dwarves; elves; an animal that
  talks; an animal that is a friend; dragon; unicorn; eagle;
  fox; wolf; snake; tiger; lion; ants; bees; winged horse;
  cunning cats; spider; hare; tortoise; crow; bird of paradise;
  faithful dog.

Objects

- ring; shoes; ten league boots; crown; invisible cloak;
  beautiful gowns; goblet or cup; golden ball; magic stone;
  charm; necklace; beans or seeds to plant; whistle; apple;
  stone animal; pendant; needle or spinning wheel; candle;
  lantern or fire; sack or bag; purse; flute.

THE LION, THE WITCH AND THE WARDROBE

This title has always intrigued me because it contains three
such disparate ingredients. I have often used this as a story
warm-up. Make a list of six wild animals, characters from
traditional tales and objects. The children throw a dice to
randomly select a title. Then see who can create the best tale
that involves all three items, e.g. *The Fox, the Woodcutter and
the Ladder*.

Wild Animals	Traditional Characters	Objects
Tiger	Witch	Mobile phone
Lion	Giant	Window
Wolf	Baker	Ladder
Fox	Princess	Door
Eagle	Farmer	Key
Snake	Woodcutter	Walking boots

STORY BOXES

This is a fun idea. Collect objects that go in a story and put these into a box; or supply every child with a shoe box and the children create little story rooms or diaramas.

STORY MUSEUMS

When I began teaching, most LEAs had a museum service that would deliver artefacts to support your topic. I borrowed a stuffed fox, Roman pottery and a Victorian coat. It's a shame that such services no longer exist, but perhaps children could collect objects, figures, puppets and images related to a story and build their own story museum.

Year 6 pupils might fill a garage box with ration books, tapes of local memories and memorabilia to accompany a book such as Michael Morpurgo's book about evacuees, *Friend or Foe*. A year 3 box about Flat Stanley would surely have an enormous envelope in it! Year 1 pupils might collect a slipper, a cloak, a pumpkin and a clock to represent Cinderella. 'Story museum displays' could be used as a strategy for representing and revisiting stories using a visual and auditory approach. They could be displayed in class or set out in the hall or reception for other classes. 'Story Museums' might make stories more meaningful and memorable if they provide a tangible representation of a tale – a ball of string, a maze, a bull's horn and a rock painted red could represent *Theseus and the Minotaur*!

STORY CONSEQUENCES

We used to play this game at Christmas and one year it struck me that it actually might help to create the bare bones of a story. Supply each child with a strip of paper. They write on it and fold it over, then pass the paper on. The last person unfolds the paper and there is the bare bones of the story – which can then be retold and embellished. The story will always have a similar format – character X meets character Y in a certain place. Something has gone wrong. He speaks to her and she replies. The problem is solved. Here are the instructions I use – though do experiment with alternative versions:

Adjective to describe a man	Tall
Name of a male character	Gandalf
Adjective to describe a woman	Tiny
Name of a female character	Mother Hubbard
Where they met	Under the Troll's bridge
The problem	A bank robbery
He said to her	Can you see the fishing boats?
She said to him	My handbag has gone
What happened next	They ran into the sea
How they solved the dilemma	The called in the army

CHANGING A STORY BY SIMPLE SUBSTITUTIONS

Once children know a story well, ask them to retell it but alter basic names such as characters, places and objects.

Once upon a time there was a little girl called Little Yellow Hoodie. One day her uncle said, 'Take this basket of food to your Grandad.' . . .

CHANGE A STORY WITH ONE MODERN ITEM

The challenge here is to take a well-known story and retell it but insert a modern item. For instance, ask the children to retell 'Little Red Riding Hood', but she has a mobile phone. How does this alter what happens?

CHANGING A STORY BY EMBELLISHING

When children know a simple tale well, they can begin to develop it by embellishing the tale:

- By adding in more description, e.g.:

    The little goat paused. The bridge looked rickety and he wasn't sure if it would hold his weight. Carefully, he began to trot across but the planks of wood creaked and groaned. Halfway across he had the shock of his life because . . .

- adding in more dialogue, e.g.:

    'Who goes trip-trap trip-trap over my bridge?' asked the Troll. 'Why it's that skinny goat from over the hill. So what do you want young 'un?'

- adding in a new character, e.g.:

    Goldilocks turned to Josie and told her to try the small bowl of porridge because there was plenty left . . .

- adding in new incidents or modernising the tale, e.g.:

    Goldilocks flicked on the TV and settled down to watch Neighbours . . .

CHANGING A STORY BY MAKING DRAMATIC ALTERATIONS

This form of retelling begins to move away from the original of a story. The children retell the tale but make some big changes that actually alter what happens within the tale:

- altering characters, e.g. so that a good character becomes greedy;

- altering settings, e.g. so that a character journeys through a housing estate rather than a forest;
- altering the way the story opens or ends;
- altering the mood – retell *The Three Bears* but build up the suspense;
- altering events but sticking to the basic plot.

One way to make this playful is by providing specific instructions such as, 'Retell the story of the Billy Goats Gruff but instead of goats have snowmen'.

CHANGING A STORY BY ALTERING THE VIEWPOINT

This could mean retelling a tale from a different character's viewpoint. For instance, Mr Wolf might be asked for his version of events; or a well-known tale might be retold as a letter, diary entry, news bulletin or mobile phone call, e-mail or text message. To summarise, altering the viewpoint could mean:

- retelling from a different character's view;
- retelling in a different form (text type) – as a letter, diary entry, etc.;
- retelling in a totally new setting, e.g. Billy Goats Gruff in a city;
- retelling in a different time, e.g. Cinderella in modern times;
- retelling in a different genre, e.g. retelling a traditional tale as a thriller. e.g.:

Goldy froze. She had heard the door handle give the slightest squeak and could see that it was steadily turning. Somebody was trying to get in! She ducked under the table and kept quite still.

'SUPPOSING' OR 'WHAT IF?'

When developing story plots and ideas, try using the 'what if' or 'supposing' strategy. A good game is to develop the habit of creating simple story ideas by brainstorming together lists of unusual and crazy ideas using 'supposing' or 'what if' as a starting point. Ask children to think on their own or in pairs and then generate lots of ideas. For instance, here is a simple menu of 'supposings' to stimulate sci-fi story ideas:

Supposing. . . you travel to a new planet and

- cannot get back to the space ship;
- have to rescue a prisoner.

Supposing. . . pollution has almost ruined the world and

- robots rule – but a small band of humans are left.

Supposing. . . friendly aliens visit our world but

- one is left behind and is in danger of being captured by a greedy zoo keeper.

Supposing. . . someone invents

- a time travel machine;
- a robot that is exactly like a human but becomes evil;
- a robot that does the opposite of what it should do;
- a computer that hypnotises people.

Supposing. . . you live in a future age when

- humans are enslaved to cruel aliens;
- cruel robots rule the Earth;
- a small band of humans tries to start a new colony on a hostile world.

USING BASIC PLOTS

Over the years there has been much discussion about basic plots. Many are mixtures. One game is to categorise titles or traditional tales. Another would be to just rehearse mapping out the story mountains for different basic plots. The main ones that I seem to find are as follows:

1. Cumulative, e.g. *The Very Hungry Caterpillar*.
2. Problem / resolution, e.g. *Stormbreaker*
3. Warning, e.g. *The Minpins*
4. Quest, e.g. *Lord of the Rings*
5. Wishing, e.g. *The Three Wishes*
6. Lost / found, e.g. *The Hobbit*
7. Defeating the monster, e.g. *Jack and the Beanstalk*
8. Cinderella, e.g. *James and the Giant Peach*
9. Magical – place, events, powers, e.g. *Harry Potter*
10. Character flaw, e.g. *Horrid Henry*
11. Jokes, e.g. *Captain Underpants*

It was Samuel Johnson who suggested that 'the same images, with very little variation, have served all the authors who have ever written'. If we take one of the basic plots and look more carefully, you may see how the idea works. The 'warning story' is one such simple pattern. This tale type hinges around a warning being ignored.

The pattern lends itself to warnings about local places that might be dangerous – car dumps, a quarry, a cliff or an old tin mine. Begin the story with a warning: *'Don't fool around by the canal,' snapped Mrs Jenkins . . . '.* The two main characters set off, deciding to ignore what they have been told. They head for the forbidden setting, but on arrival disaster soon strikes, with one of the characters in trouble. Now a rescue attempt is called for, followed by an ending in which the original 'warner' reappears: *'I thought I told you not to . . . '.*

The warning itself acts as a trigger that focuses the ensuing action. Macbeth met witches, Alice met a rabbit, Aladdin met a sorcerer – all of these events trigger their tales. Another similar strategy is to begin by introducing a key fear that the main character will then meet and eventually overcome: *Billy had always been afraid of being trapped in the darkness...* Again, the opening foreshadows the tale.

USING STORY PROBLEMS

The idea is that the children roll dice or select from a hat a story problem and have to tell a short story in one minute based around the problem.

1. Everything is OK but then an intruder arrives.
2. The main character is warned not to do something but does it nevertheless.
3. The main character has a secret.
4. The main character tells a lie.
5. The main character has a flaw – is greedy, jealous, mean, etc.
6. The main character is afraid of someone or something.
7. Two contrasting characters disagree.
8. The main character has a dream that starts to come true.
9. The main character has to hide or hide something.
10. The main character is chased.
11. Someone does something wrong.
12. There is a problem.
13. The main character is picked on.
14. Someone wishes for something.
15. Someone gets their wish but it is spoiled/stolen/lost.
16. Someone is sent on a journey to get or deliver something.
17. Everything is OK until a monster/something nasty appears.
18. Someone wakes up and has turned into something else or another person, e.g. their teacher.
19. Someone is sick and the main character has to make a dangerous journey to fetch a cure.
20. Something precious is lost.

RIDDLING QUEST

Sketch a map that has many hostile features – swamp, snake pit, chasm, shark pool, etc. Set the children a task to invent a quest in which a traveller crosses this landscape but at some point meets a monster. There is a riddling contest. Below are some riddles to use. Collect or invent more.

A hill full, a hole full but you cannot catch a bowlful.

What flies forever and takes rest never?

The more you feed it, the more it grows high. But give it a drink and it will die!

What has an eye but can see nothing?

What walks on four legs in the morning, on two legs at noon, and in the evening goes on three?

The more it dries, the wetter it gets.

What always goes up but never comes down?

Answers:
Smoke; Wind; Fire; Potato; Man – crawls as a baby, then walks on two legs – till finally, uses a stick as an old person so has three legs; Towel; Age.

A RIDDLING YARN

This story is a great one to set as a problem riddle for a class. Can they work out the answer?

Story: A man went to a fair where he bought a goat, a wolf and a cabbage. On the way home he had to cross the river. He can only take them over one by one as the boat is too small. He cannot leave the goat and the cabbage alone or the goat will eat the cabbage. He cannot leave the wolf and the goat for a similar reason. How can he get all three across the river?

Answer: take the goat across. Go back and fetch the cabbage. Return with the goat, leaving the cabbage behind. Now take the wolf across, leaving the goat behind. Leave the wolf with the cabbage and return for the goat.

ENDLESS STORY

Use this as a basis for inventing new endless stories. Instead of sheep, some children have used ants, locusts, rats, bats, cats, dogs and bees.

Once there was a shepherd who could tell when it would snow. When the snow was miles away, he only had to taste the wind and he knew how long he had to fetch the sheep down from the hills.

One winter, he woke in the middle of the night, sniffed the cold air and knew that a great snowstorm would cover the valley. So, soon he was striding over the dark hills, whistling all the sheep down.

Now to get into the sheep pens, they had to pass over a small stile. First one sheep passed through. 'There she goes,' muttered the shepherd. Then another passed through. 'There she goes,' muttered the shepherd. Then another sheep passed through. 'There she goes,' muttered the shepherd. (*Keep this going until the children get fed up!*) And as far as I know he is still there, seeing all his sheep through to safety, one by one, one by one, one by one.

THE STORY CIRCLE GAME

Recently, I have been trying to write a play by e-mail with the playwright and poet Joseph Coelho. We send each other a line at a time – the dialogue bouncing back and forth. He sent me these workshop ideas that he uses in school:

All participants stand in a circle. I tell the group that I will take them on an adventure using just sound and movement, which they must copy. I then begin by enacting a series of sounds and movements such as opening a creaking chest and taking something out, and then having that thing grow or shrink or turn into a mode of transport that takes me elsewhere. I will do this for about a minute or two. The movements and sounds are entirely improvised but there is no reason why they could not be prepared beforehand, especially if you want to explore a specific genre.

So a horror story might start by opening a creaking door, an action-adventure might start by hanging off a cliff. Once finished, I ask the children what happened and make it clear that there is no right or wrong. I try to get as many different interpretations for various parts of the story as possible.

During this process, I will also encourage the children to give details. For instance, if they say we were on a motorbike, I will say, 'What colour was the bike?' Or if they say, 'We were in a jungle', I'll say, 'What did you see in the jungle?' I then invite one of the children to take us on an adventure. We repeat the process of copying them and discussing what we think happened.

Once everyone has had a turn, the children can be sent off and asked to write down their favourite story. I often give the children a blank comic book template of five blank squares and ask them to write their story in comic book form. Those five squares can be treated as five scenes, or five paragraphs, of a play or story. For scenes, I use another template that sets out the structure of a scene, i.e. scene number at top, character name on left-hand side, dialogue tabbed in, action in square brackets etc.

83

FIVE-POINT STORY ARC

Joseph also recommended this workshop.

Using a pared-down version of the eight-point story arc, I will show the children how every story fits the arc normally through an example they all know (Spiderman is a favourite) and write down the arc on the board as follows.

1. Routine – what the character does every day
2. Desire – What does the character want or need?
3. Obstacle – What stops the character from getting what they want or need?
4. Resolution – How does the character overcome their obstacle?
5. What has the character learned?

I will then lead the group through an example by first creating a character with them. I do this by asking three simple questions:

1. Is the character a boy or a girl?
2. What is their personality like?
3. What do they do?

I will then take the character through each step of the arc with the children, taking their suggestions to progress the story. Once I have gone through the example, I will ask the children to create their own in groups using the comic book.

THE SUN AND MOON

I have known the poet and storyteller John Rice for about 35 years. John, Brian Moses and myself used to give readings and perform in clubs and schools. He recently sent me these ideas for storytelling workshops:

- Two partners: boy and girl who become Sun and Moon.
- They improvise a story, 'Sun's Big Day Out!', telling it one word at a time. It is slow and boring so the first thing they

learn is that they need to plan a story before it will be of interest to anyone.

- Sun and Moon then plan a ghost story and tell it one sentence at a time. This is much better. There is a sense of story already beginning to develop.
- Sun and Moon match up with another Sun and Moon duo to plan, create and tell four chapters of a murder mystery. This is where planning, storyboarding, the creation of characters and the division of labour begin to show. The four performers tell but do not act or perform.
- This time we need to build in performance so the next task for the foursome is to devise and act out a spy thriller (James Bond action movie is best). The audience does the theme tune and sound effects for each performance. There must be a lot of action and all the usual Bond-type stuff – fast cars, explosions, gadgets, pretty girls, a potential world dominator etc. It's all great fun.
- But this is not about doing a play, so cut back on the action and return to actual storytelling. This time it's back to the Sun and Moon twosome and the theme this time is a faery story. Notice it's not a *fairy* story but a story from the World of Faery where Good is in constant combat with Evil. Explore the dark side!
- Throughout the entire warm-up, the audience must be supportive and allowed to 'direct' the storytellers so that their telling skills and performances improve incrementally. Set a benchmark and encourage or challenge the performers to continually improve.

NURSERY RHYME GAME

I have played this game with key stage 3 children and they seemed to enjoy the anarchy of the idea. Take a well-known nursery rhyme and tell the story. This could be a straight retelling or it might be retold in another genre so that 'Little Miss Muffet' becomes a horror story. Rhymes that lend themselves to this treatment are – 'Humpty Dumpty', 'Sing a Song of Sixpence', 'Lucy Locket', 'Three Blind Mice', 'Little

Jack Horner', 'Jack Spratt', 'Simple Simon', 'Mary's Lamb', 'Hey Diddle Diddle', 'Goosey Goosey Gander' and 'Little Miss Muffet'.

STORY SHORTS

The idea of this game is very simple. Present a story in its bare form. The children then work in pairs to develop a full telling, adding in detail, description, characterisation and so on. Drawing a map first, walking the steps and retelling in pairs to gain fluency, confidence and to allow the story to develop are all important parts of the process. You can ask them to tell it in about one minute and then retell it in two minutes and so on. What you will find is that as they become familiar with the plot, they begin to embellish and gain confidence. Here are some 'story shorts' to get you started:

Story 1
Once there was a poor boy who loved drawing but had no pencil. In a dream he is given a magic brush. Whatever he paints comes true. He is told only to use it for good. He helps the villagers with things like a new plough. The greedy king orders him to draw gold. He draws a distant island of gold and a boat. The king sets sail. The boy draws a storm and the greedy king is never seen again.

Story 2
A fisherman catches a huge fish and sets it free because it is so beautiful. It is the king of the fishes and says that it can grant him one wish at midnight. The fisherman does not know what to wish for. His father is blind and needs eyesight. His family are very poor, and he longs for a baby. At midnight he returns to the sea's edge and manages to get all he wishes for in one by asking 'for my father to see our baby in a cradle made of gold'.

Story 3
A boy has to look after the sheep each day on the hillside. His father tells him to call for help if a wolf appears. He keeps

calling for help because he thinks it funny to see the villagers running up the hill. One day a wolf does appear and he calls for help but everyone ignores him. The sheep get eaten and the boy learns a lesson.

Story 4

King Minos throws Daedalus and his son Icarus into a tower because he blames Daedalus for the death of his son, the Minotaur. Daedalaus makes a plan to escape. He gathers feathers and candle wax and makes two pairs of wings. They fly from the tower. Icarus flies too near the sun, his wings melt and he falls to his doom.

Story 5

A farmer finds a little pixie. He asks the pixie to show him where all his gold is hidden. The pixie says he will, but warns the farmer to return home because the cows are in the corn, the sheep have escaped and the roof has blown off. The farmer thinks this is a trick. They go to the wood and the pixie shows the farmer the tree under which he has buried his pixie gold. The farmer needs a spade. He ties his blue scarf round the tree, sets the pixie free and runs home. He is met by disasters but gets a spade and runs back. However, every tree has a blue scarf round it so he never finds his treasure.

Story 6

The prince leaves his faithful dog in charge of the baby and sets off hunting. On returning he finds the dog covered in blood and the cradle knocked over with no sign of the baby. Thinking the dog has eaten the baby, he kills it. As the dog dies, he hears a noise from under a blanket. He pulls it back to find the baby alive and a dead wolf beside it!

Story 7

A dragon is ruining the countryside. The king asks for help. No-one can defeat the monster. A cobbler claims he can. Everyone laughs. The cobbler sews together cow skins and stuffs them with gunpowder, sulphur and hot spices. He drags them to the dragon's den and throws them in. The dragon thinks they are a meal and eats them. The meal is so hot that the dragon flies to the river and drinks until it bursts!

Story 8

The cruel north wind and the sun have a contest to see who is the strongest. They decide to see who can make a farmer in the fields take his coat off. First the north wind blows hard and colder and colder. But the colder it blows, the more firmly the farmer pulls on his coat. Then the sun turns up the heat. Within a few minutes, the farmer is sweating and takes off his coat.

HODJA TALES

There are hundreds of witty tales about Mulla Nasrudin, a Persian trickster and wise man. Here are a few short ones. The idea is similar to the above game. The children retell the tale but embellish and draw the story out.

a. Crossing the river

The Hodja came to the edge of a huge river. He was desperate to cross to the other side.
Several days later some people from the town found him pulling the bridge down. They asked, 'Why are you pulling the bridge down?'
The Hodja stopped and replied, 'So, I can build a raft to cross over, of course!'

b. Speed limit

The Hodja was driving his car as fast as he could go. When the police eventually stopped him, they asked him why he was driving as if the Devil was on his coat tails.
'I'm driving quickly so that I can get home before I have a crash,' he replied.

c. The cliff

One day the Hodja climbed right to the very top of a high cliff. From there he could see right across the whole country.

He slipped at the edge and fell right down to the bottom. Everyone gathered round to see if he was alright. 'What happened?' someone asked him.

'I don't know,' replied the Hodja, 'I've only just got here myself.'

URBAN LEGENDS

Pupils at key stage 3 have an avid interest in urban legends. These can be swapped and retold. They can be developed into full-length 'tellings'. Here I have presented some as 'story shorts'. The game is to retell but embellish into a proper story.

Legend 1
A fire crew rescue a cat from a tree. The old lady is so grateful she makes them tea. As they leave, they reverse the fire engine over the cat!

Legend 2
In preparation for the Olympics, a high diver visits the local pool every night to practise. One night all the lights are out, so he reckons there has been a power cut. He climbs the high board, stretches out his arms and is about to dive. At that moment, in the semi-darkness he sees his shadow on the opposite wall shaped like a cross. He kneels and prays. As he is doing this, the caretaker returns and switches the electricity back on. The high diver opens his eyes and looks down. The pool was empty as it was being cleaned!

Legend 3
A man was driving home when he had a flat tyre. He changed the tyre and then carefully drove on. Just round the bend was a 20-car pile-up that he would have driven into. A tornado had sucked up thousands of toads from a nearby lake and deposited them on the road making it dangerously slippery!

Legend 4

A traveller returns from south America. A lump appears on his arm. In the end he goes to the doctor. It is full of tiny spiders.

Legend 5

A traveller befriends a cat in Bali and has it shipped home. When it arrives, the cat attacks the traveller's dog and kills it. It turns out that it wasn't a cat but an enormous water rat.

Legend 6

A girl is given a new mobile phone for her birthday. She opens all her presents. She cannot find the phone so they ring it from the house phone. They hear the phone ringing – from inside the dog!

Older pupils enjoy telling and writing such stories. They have a macabre and jokey element to them that appeals. See resources for a suggested collection.

BURGER PLANS

Many children find planning writing difficult. It can be tedious. When writing stories, planning too much may take the adventure out of the writing. As Nico (aged 7) said to me, 'What I like about writing is that you never quite know what is going to happen'.

In one school I visited, the children were using 'burger plans' – a simple and appealing idea that the children enjoyed using. The top and bottom halves of the bun provide a space for the children to write in ideas for their opening and ending. These are left quite large so that the children can note specific phrases. The layers in the middle of the burger represent different paragraphs. Year 3 children might only have one or two layers, whilst more proficient writers may have more.

The teacher has to show the children how to plan using the burger, and then how to turn the 'burger plan' into writing. It is a simple idea, effective at improving organisation in writing – and the children enjoy using it. As one boy said to me, 'It makes for tasty writing'!

CHAPTER 7

Twenty things to do with a story

This section is a series of activities that help children engage with stories, deepening their understanding and enjoyment. It is really a checklist of possibilities. You are working with a story, what sorts of activities might help children deepen their understanding? The activities you choose depend upon the story and what is needed. Many of these ideas are drama-based. It is worth loitering with a story so that the children really get to know it well. In our educational climate of 'delivery' mode of a 'curriculum', teachers may feel under pressure to 'get through' units of work and ensure 'coverage' – sometimes at the expense of learning and progress.

ART

Paint or draw key scenes from a story. Display these in a line to show the sequence of the story or as a book. Make models of key objects.

ROLE PLAY

Identify a scene and role play what happens. Pause at a key moment and role play – then read/tell the next part of the story.

FREE ROLE PLAY

Provide a play area such as a bears' cave or Grandma's cottage complete with dressing-up clothes that acts as a simple invitation to 'play at' the story.

SAND STORIES

Put models in the sand area for children to use when making up stories as part of their play.

HOT SEATING

A volunteer in role as a story character takes the hot seat and is questioned by class mates.

PUPPET THEATRE

Finger puppets and a mini theatre should be used for children to play at the story, retelling it or inventing new ideas using the same characters.

AGONY AUNTS

A character visits an agony aunt or phones into a radio programme for advice.

STATEMENTS TO POLICE

A wrongdoer from a story is questioned by the police for their account of events.

TRIALS

Have the teacher in role as judge. Children work as solicitors to defend or accuse a character, e.g. the Iron Man for wrecking the countryside. Characters from the story can be called to explain what has happened.

ROLE ON THE WALL

Someone lies down on sheets of paper – an outline is drawn plus comments, quotes, suggestions.

TV INTERVIEWS

In role as journalists, interview a character from a story. Follow up by presenting this as a broadcast using a digital camera or by writing a news story for a local paper.

STORY SALE

Choose an object from a story and write a 'For Sale' notice, e.g. *For Sale – The Minotaur's Horn. Straight from the labyrinth, the genuine article...*

LIKES, DISLIKES, PUZZLES AND PATTERNS

Put children into pairs to make a list about a story or poem of likes, dislikes, puzzles and patterns. Or, each pair makes a list of five questions they are curious about. Later on, list these as a class and see if other pairs can provide ideas or answers.

STORY POEM

Stop at a vivid moment in a story. Use a simple frame (*I heard..., I saw..., I touched..., I wondered...*) to write a senses poem in role as a character in the story, e.g.:

I heard the distant rumble of the Minotaur's hot breath.
I heard the dark hooves scraping the sandy floor.
I heard the heavy beat of my heart as it drew nearer.

I saw the sudden sharp flash of its red eyes glinting in the darkness.
I saw the ragged hair and the flared nostrils.

I touched the cold walls for comfort.
I touched the thin string of Ariadne's hope.

I wondered if my fear would turn into dust. . .

PHONE A FRIEND

Sit the children back-to-back and let them pretend to make a mobile phone call. One of them is in role as a character in a story – or witness to a key event – and the other might be a relative.

MIMING SCENES

Mime a story. Can the rest of the class guess the story? This could be done individually, in pairs or as story circles.

MEETINGS

Hold a meeting of villagers or townsfolk to discuss and perhaps vote upon what should be done.

GOSSIP

Two bystanders gossip about events in a story or what a character has been up to.

RECORD IT

As we become more comfortable with technology it should be simple enough to make audio CDs and DVDs of children telling stories. These could be made by older pupils for younger ones to take home as a bedtime story to be listened to or watched. Also, a class collection might be sold to parents and well-wishers.

THOUGHTS IN THE HEAD

Draw a cartoon and thought bubble for a character in a story or develop a monologue to say aloud.

CHAPTER 8
Story reading detectives

I was in a school in Scunthorpe and the year 6 teacher was telling me about her children's reading. The problem was 'inference and deduction'. I'm not often given to moments of blinding revelation but on this occasion I had a sudden idea – quick-fire reading games could provide daily practice, just to hone up reading skills that would then be used on complete texts. The games would only take a few minutes, could be presented on PowerPoint and be an ideal way to start a session with everyone involved. Since then I have invented about 20 games – and other teachers are thanking Scunthorpe for that moment of insight!

I built the games around the strands in the new primary framework for literacy as well as the article on reading comprehension that appears on the Standards website. Once you are familiar with the games, keep playing them by substituting different snippets of text or words, upping or lowering the level of challenge to suit the needs of your class. Demonstrate how to play the games so the children hear you thinking your comprehension processes aloud.

Of course, we will be reading the daily class novel and working with whole stories, poems and non-fiction texts. But using extracts for quick-fire skills practice could provide a snappy strategy for fine-tuning reading skills that can then be applied to whole books, deepening understanding and appreciation.

SPOT THE KEY POINTS

Provide a short passage. The children have to find the main facts, e.g. Can you find three facts in 30 seconds?

> Michael Morpurgo, author of over 60 books, likes to take his dog Bercelet for walks at Nethercott Farm, which is one of the three 'Farms for City Children'.

DEDUCE THE CHARACTER'S FEELINGS

Read the passage. How is the character feeling, remembering that there might be several ideas? List the clues. This game needs a short passage in which how a character feels is not directly stated.

> Fiona glared through the railings at the cars as they swished by. She hunched her shoulders, bunched her fists and waited, tapping her foot. . .

READING DETECTIVES

Provide a short extract or sentence. The children have to be 'reading detectives' and list clues that suggest something that is not directly stated. For instance, what do the clues suggest about this character?

> Miss Groan strode into the classroom. She took one look at 3B and there was silence. No one breathed. Even the gerbil stopped pedalling on his treadwheel.

PREDICTING THE CONSEQUENCES

Read a passage through. What might be the result of what has happened? List possibilities.

Barry was in the middle of painting the book cover to his favourite book when Cody came into the classroom. He was covered in mud and smelt rather nasty. As soon as he saw Barry, he let out a bark, wagged his tail, and took a flying leap on to the art table . . .

WORD MEANINGS

Write down a sentence with a 'hard' word in it – list possible alternatives. Which one is closest? Use a thesaurus to help you.

Tracy **sneered** as Jodie tried on her new, glittery hair band. 'You look like a baby,' she snapped.

Does **'sneered'** mean: scoffed, mocked, sniggered, giggled, jeered.

SEQUENCE

You can play 'sequencing' in various ways. Take one sentence and muddle the words; or take a short paragraph and muddle the sentences. This example might be handy for discussing the notion of topic sentences:

- Their proper diet consists of leaves, twigs and fruit but they can be tempted by a doughnut.
- They eat about 150 kilograms of food every day.
- Surprisingly for such a large animal, they only have four teeth for grinding and chewing their food.
- Elephants eat a lot.

99

QUESTION AND STATEMENT

Read a short passage. What do you *know* and what can you deduce? Make three statements about what you know and list several questions.

> Barry and Sally were both in our class. But no-one ever spoke to them. They were both snobs. They lived on the posh estate and walked to school together like goody-goodies. I reckoned that they both thought they were better than the rest of us.

IN ONE WORD

Read a paragraph and then decide on one word that could act as a title. For instance, this paragraph might be called 'Escape':

> The two boys dashed out of the cave and began to run up the beach. They could hear the old man shouting and yelling behind them but they were not going to stop for him or anyone else. As soon as they reached the sea road, they leapt on to the bikes and cycled back to the town as fast as they could. No-one could catch them now!

COMPARE OPENINGS

Read these openings. Which book would you choose to read and why? Find the 'hook' that the author uses to intrigue the reader. What is it about the opening that makes you think that it is the sort of book you like reading?

- Reluctantly, Skater picked up his schoolbag.
- His name was Toy Jubilee and he was the largest person that I had ever met. My Grandfather had warned me not to hang around with Toy but that made it even more tempting.
- The message was written in earth writing but none of the crew could read it.

WHAT WILL THEY SAY NEXT?

Provide something one character says. What do you think the reply will be?

'Why do you want to run in the race when you know that you will be beaten?'

CHANGED WORDS

This game is a form of 'cloze procedure'. Write out a sentence or two. Alter some of the words so that it becomes funny or non-sensical. The children have to decide which words have been altered and change them back to what they think they were originally.

Jazzy turned to her imaginary doughnut and potatoed. To her porridge the ghostly shape potatoed back. Jazzy pineappled. That had never primrosed before.

Original version:

(Jazzy turned to her imaginary friend and winked. To her surprise the ghostly shape winked back. Jazzy gasped. That had never happened before.)

CHAPTER 9

Creating a storymaking climate in school and classroom

This section is about developing a story reading culture as well as storytelling. The more children read stories, the stronger their storytelling and writing will be because they will be drawing on a more powerful bank of images, ideas and language. Storytelling cannot replace story reading – we need both to flourish.

According to a 'YouGov' survey (2005), reported in *Reading for Pleasure: A Research Overview* by Christina Clarke and Kate Rumbold (NLT, 2006), 53 per cent of parents claim that they read daily to their children before starting school. This drops to 34 per cent between the ages of 5 and 8 and down to 23 per cent between 8 and 12. How can we encourage families and children to read more and what can we do in school to promote reading?

Pleasure makes reading habit-forming. And we know that pupils who read for pleasure are more likely to succeed in school. So we have to build communities where reading is enjoyed as a central aspect of school and home life. Over the last few years, I have been lucky enough to visit many schools where children love reading. Increasingly, I am visiting schools where storytelling is also flourishing. The National Literacy Trust website is a great source of ideas for promoting reading, some of which I mention in this chapter. Here are some of the ideas I have seen being used.

1. BRING BACK THE DAILY CLASS READER

It was Marilyn Jaeger Adams, the American reading guru, who said in her 1990 book *Beginning to Read: Thinking and Learning about Print* (MIT Press, 1990):

> The single most important activity for building the knowledge and skills eventually required for reading appears to be reading aloud to children regularly and interactively.

A recent survey carried out by the *Times Educational Supplement* showed that the daily class reader was not a common feature of most primary schools – especially at key stage 2. But if we do not read to the children, we can be fairly sure that for many children no-one else will.

The class reader is one of the key ways in which we tempt children into reading. It is the prime way in which we establish a 'reading climate' – by putting them through the imaginative challenge of engaging with good literature. New authors can be introduced and books read that are beyond the children's decoding level. The teacher models enthusiasm and interpretation, savouring the narrative. If we want children to write well then they need to hear what good writing sounds like! The Primary Strategy calls this, the 'Read Aloud Programme'.

2. INTRODUCE DAILY STORYTELLING

Some schools now include daily storytelling as a routine across key stage 1. They aim to build up a bank of well-known tales as well as developing the ability to innovate and invent new stories. At key stage 2 many schools are ensuring that children work on a told story each half-term. In this way, children would have retold and developed a bank of some 50 stories by the time they leave primary school.

3. ESTABLISH A LITERATURE SPINE

Who are the key poets and authors that children should experience? Which are the stories and poems that all children should meet? Some schools have created a 'literature spine' that identifies the key texts that will be read each year. This ensures that children meet the great classics, from *The Iron Man* to *Tom's Midnight Garden*. Knowing the key texts also means that resources can be gathered (half-class sets of key readers and bunches of five of other books). These collections can be supplemented with autobiographical detail, videos and material downloaded from author websites.

4. IDENTIFY MENTOR TEXTS

The next step is to identify a few stories or books each year that will become key mentor texts – texts that will be often referred to as a frame of reference for writing – *Do you remember how Anne Fine started 'Bill's new Frock' – perhaps we could use that same approach here?* Which books, short stories or picture books could act as mentor texts? For instance, the opening of *The Iron Man* (Ted Hughes) acts as a good example of:

- introduce a monster in the first line;
- use three questions to get the reader wondering;
- use a repeated answer for emphasis.

The novel begins: *The Iron Man came to the top of the cliff. How far had he walked? Nobody knows. Where had he come from? Nobody knows. How was he made? Nobody knows.*

Jake, aged 9, reused this opening in his story about a dragon: *The dragon lurched across the hills. Where was it from? No one knew. Where was it going? No one knew? What had it come for? No one knew. But they would soon find out.*

It might be possible for each year group to have one or two stories that the class know really well and are used as touchstones, reminders and a resource to draw upon to influence their writing.

5. ESTABLISH WEEKLY 'RECOMMENDATIONS'

Hold weekly 'recommendation' sessions where you introduce children to books that they might enjoy for independent reading. Children take it in turn, on a rota, to make a recommendation. They should:

- select a text that they have enjoyed and think others will enjoy;
- introduce it briefly;
- read a well-prepared section – this will motivate others to read the book.

Weekly recommendations is an important part of creating a buzz about reading. In one school, children put silver stars on the spine of books that they recommend.

6. INCREASE INDEPENDENT READING

We know that our most proficient writers are avid readers. At key stage 1, we are good at monitoring independent reading and parents are more likely to play an active role in their child's reading. Once they hit key stage 2, this falls away. It is quite possible for children to drift though key stage 2, reading very little independently. We could:

- monitor independent reading more closely;
- establish quiet independent reading after lunchtime;
- make sure we have plenty of 'quick reads';
- develop a very strong reward system for reading books;
- make sure the books that children take home are those that they can read with only a slight edge of challenge;

- reward parents/carers who support reading with badges and certificates;
- provide lunch clubs for those who cannot read at home.

7. USE OF READING LOGS

The original NLS material on reading introduced the idea of 'reading logs' but many schools have yet to establish these as a helpful strategy for developing reading. The log has in it a list of possible tasks. All the tasks need to be completed but in no particular order. Provide a strong reward for completing reading log tasks. Model and show good examples so the children know the sort of thing that is possible.

Once you have established the idea of reading log tasks as an independent activity, develop the type of task sheet so that you have tasks appropriate for less confident readers as well as more challenging activities for more able readers. Typical tasks for years 5 or 6 average readers might include:

- Draw a new cover
- Write a new blurb
- Explain the story in 50 words
- Choose an incident and write a 100 word diary entry from the viewpoint of one of the characters
- Copy the first few sentences – make a list of three reasons why it is a good/bad opening
- Rewrite the ending
- Turn an event from the story into a news report of 100 words
- Draw a family tree or cast of characters
- Turn a section of dialogue into a scene from a play
- Explain which character is most like you and why
- Explain the theme of the story in 50 words
- Write an imaginary interview with the author
- Write a letter to the main character offering advice
- Stop at a key moment and write three ideas for what might happen next

- Find a paragraph that involves either suspense, action or description – write it out, label it, identifying writing strategies.

A useful resource for developing readings would be: *Reading Adventures* by Jo Garton, published by Philip and Tacey (0845 123 7760).

8. USE ICT

We should also be building up class libraries of:

- CDs of poets reading poems;
- DVDs of authors and poets;
- hyperlinks to author sites;
- films of books.

Brian Moses edited a good CD of performance poems titled *Poems Out Loud* (Hodder Wayland, ISBN 1-84032-69-4). It contains a range of poets from different cultures and has a spine-tingling reading of 'Tyger, Tyger', read by John Agard.

I have just finished editing a series of four poetry programmes for the BBC in their excellent *Let's Write* series that began with narrative and fiction. Titled *Let's Write Poetry*, it contains video of Kit Wright reading 'The Magic Box' as well as Brian Patten, Roger McGough, Paul Cookson, Val Bloom and Michael Rosen ('Chocolate Cake'), with dramatic readings of old favourites such as 'Jabberwocky'.

9. PROMOTE THE STORY AT BEDTIME

A few months ago I opened a library at Springhill Primary School. All the staff and most of the children wore pyjamas. Hot chocolate and marshmallows were served. Parents came and I told stories. The message was: the bedtime book is a good thing. The last time I asked a class of children how many

of them had a story at bedtime only three hands went up –
and they were year 2 children! We need to be actively
promoting family reading – workshops for parents and carers
should be an annual event. It is useful to hold sessions where
'how to share a story' is discussed as well as sessions for
different age groups where we introduce parents to different
books that are relevant to their children.

Many parents are not sure which books to borrow from the
library or to buy for their children. Perhaps we need to work
more closely with children's librarians to produce booklists of
good independent reads for different age groups, good books
to read to your child, genre lists, suggested books as birthday
presents and good reads for boys (pirates, mysteries,
adventures, fantasy, sci-fi, etc).

10. MAKE READING VISIBLE

Keep your eye out for posters and images of males reading.
Pin these up in central areas. Use the digital camera to take
photos of members of staff reading, and display them. Take
photos in 'silhouette' and pin these up with a competition –
can you guess our mystery reader?

The National Literacy Trust suggest the idea of pinning up
photos of children taking part in 'extreme reading'. They take
a photo of themselves reading in the most 'extreme' place – in
another country, up a tree, going down a slide at Alton
Towers! 'Extreme reading' photos of members of staff could
be used as screensavers – just for everyone's amusement.

Hold reading assemblies in which teachers talk about their
reading. Invite male role models into the school to talk at
assembly about reading in their leisure and work (firemen
always seem to be a hit!). Pin up lists of 'Desert Island Books'
compiled by classes as well as adults.

11. PLAY BOOK GAMES

Instead of *X Factor*, hold *The Book Factor*. Children volunteer to talk on behalf of a book. They have to introduce the book, argue on its behalf, and can read an extract to try to persuade the audience that their choice is the best. Another version of this game would be to play *I'm a Roald Dahl Book – Get Me Out of Here*. In this game, the children have to represent a book or author who has been trapped in the jungle. Again, they have to persuade the audience that they are the one to be let out. Or the panel of book lovers could be set questions about stories by the rest of the class or teacher and a 'story quiz' could determine who escapes.

What about 'speed reading'? Half the class chooses a favourite book and sits at different places in the hall. The others are asked to move from person to person every four minutes. In that time the 'speed reader' has to persuade them that their book is the one to have a 'reading date' with, by promoting the book and reading an extract. End with a vote and the children are paired up with their book choice for a reading date!

12. USE TV AND FILM LINKS

We need to keep an eye open for TV and film links. Occasionally, a 'good' book is filmed – such as *Charlotte's Web* which is a classic and should be read to all key stage 2 children. Let's not be snooty about trashy *Doctor Who* annuals and books based on the latest craze. If the children are into it then the cunning teacher will capitalise on their enthusiasm. It is always worth dropping into children's bookshops to see what is selling.

My best find recently is the cartoon of *Howl's Moving Castle*. This is a beautiful and amazing video that could be used with a year 5/6 class rather like a novel, watching ten minutes or so at a time. The images are beautiful and the story rich in possibilities for discussion, drama and writing in role. It is based upon Dianne Wynne Jones's excellent novel of the same name.

In the same vein we need to keep children fed with story tapes, videos and CD-ROMs as well as tapping into the internet.

13. STORYTELLER AND AUTHOR VISITS AND 'BOOK WEEKS'

I think that every child should be entitled to meet an 'artist' each year – authors, poets storytellers and theatre groups. Make sure that children are familiar with the author's work and that copies of books are available for purchase, children having been forewarned to bring money.

Children should also become visiting authors themselves. Class stories, poems and information books should be published more often and become part of what is on offer for reading. Younger children can be involved in making up stories right from the start. These can be illustrated and made into Big Books for re-reading. Older pupils should be involved in creating texts on screen and, again, these can be read by others, via e-mail or placed on the school website.

14. PARENTS, CARERS AND LUNCHTIME CLUBS

We monitor home reading carefully at key stage 1 but this tails off dramatically at key stage 2. Parents tend to stop listening to their child read and stop reading to them at about year 3. We need to make sure that we work with parents through letters home, reminders at the gate, reading workshops and plenty of encouragement so that reading continues to be supported and practised daily. Reward parents and carers who support their children – 'Family Reading' badges, certificates and medals have all been tried as ways to reward and encourage parents and make reading visible and an important part of parenting.

Of course, this also means making sure that for strugglers we have plenty of 'quick reads' so that they take home books that they can manage and enjoy. In some schools teachers have identified children who for one reason or another do not receive support at home and have provided for them a reading mentor or buddy. They meet at lunchtime and the mentor listens to their mentee read and reads a book to them.

Storytelling workshops for parents and carers can be an effective and powerful tool for supporting literacy in the home. Of course, parents who lack confidence with reading may well find that telling is an avenue that they can develop with confidence. In the end, it is the story that matters – whether it is in a book or told aloud does not matter so much.

Talking of lunchtime reminds me that I always had a large store of comics, annuals and trashy books. These were read at wet playtimes and some children took them home to read. We also held book swaps rather like car boot sales.

15. READING/STORYTELLING/STORYWRITING CHAMPIONS AND ANGELS

Every school should be involved in 'Reading Champions' and 'Reading Connects', both run by the National Literacy Trust. 'Reading Champions' focuses on encouraging boys to promote reading. Lewannick CP School in Cornwall was the 'Reading Champions' Primary School of the Year in 2006. Jacqui Maynard, the school librarian, says that the 'most important thing I've learnt is to make anything the Champions do visible'. She says that the main problem was that boys lacked confidence and had yet to discover materials that they might enjoy. The boys run the group and have come up with many of their own ideas for promoting reading amongst boys. Activities they have run in school so far include:

- buddy reading with younger boys;
- the Reading Agency's Summer Challenge;

- a balloon debate about reading material;
- graphic reviews in the library;
- 'Reading Champion' themed displays;
- a top 100 favourite reads from staff and pupils;
- a quiz on the top 100 books;
- a book group;
- swap-a-book sessions.

The school's SAT results now show boys above the national average in English. For more information contact Sarah Osborne at sara.osborne@literacytrust.org.uk or log on to www.readingchampions.org.uk and scan the website. Every school should be running Reading Champions, promoting and supporting boys and girls as readers and writers. Reading Champion schools show that we can make a difference and create cultures where reading is cool. Some schools run 'Reading Champions' and also have 'Reading Angels' for girls who promote reading. It would be interesting to now move into thinking about whether we can use similar tactics to promote writing amongst boys.

'Reading Connects' provides a simple framework for developing reading across the school. It is a useful management tool that helps a school evaluate where they are and plan which areas to focus upon next. If you are engaged in focusing on improving reading already, then you have probably already tackled many of the aspects that come under the banner of 'Reading Connects'. Log on to www.readingconnects.org.uk for more information.

16. WORLD BOOK DAY

Just a quick thought. The £1 books that go on sale on World Book Day would make ideal sets of quick reads. Ideal for whole-class reading – and cheap too! Or, buy up sets of six copies and use them for guided reading. Over the years you could collect quite a bunch.

17. PUBLISH CHILDREN'S STORIES

Children's writing should be turned into mini books, anthologies, displayed on walls and in classroom scrapbooks. Younger pupils should have their words turned into mini readers to take home. Record stories and poems for other classes and sell CDs of children's performances to parents. Children should be in the habit of telling stories to other classes.

With photocopying and the computer all this is easy enough but it is still rare to find publishing of writing as a regular activity. It is worth making the effort, as you will be providing a genuine audience for the children's writing.

18. CELEBRATE AND REWARD YOUNG STORYMAKERS

Establish strategies to create a 'Storymaking School':

• regular performance and recording
• reward system for stortelling
• certificates
• posters
• screen savers
• letters/postcards home
• badges
• pencils
• journals
• books

Develop a 'storymaking is cool' culture:

• storytelling club
• storytelling festivals
• story cloaks and hats
• develop story castles and corners
• record story music
• give each class a magic story carpet

113

- use story bags and boxes
- community tales of school days
- writing café
- school website
- anthologies of children's stories
- story swaps with schools in other parts of the world
- story 'bags' and boxes
- family story project
- extreme storytelling

FINALLY

It will be our enthusiasm for stories and books and for children as readers that is the most powerful strategy for encouraging storytelling and reading. Enthusiasm is like wild fire – it spreads. Let's take the time to have a concerted effort on motivating children to tell stories, to read more and to read for pleasure. That will be a gateway to lifelong enjoyment as well as the path to educational success. The more children read, the more stories they retell, the more they become 'living anthologies'. It is this vibrant storehouse – the internal library – that helps children create, tell and write their own stories. You cannot create out of nothing. Stories develop a potent inner world that will both sustain us when life darkens and bind us together as one world people. They are beacons of hope that illuminate our world.

CHAPTER 10

Resources

The hardest aspect of storymaking is not so much the children being able to learn, retell and invent stories, but whether the busy classroom teacher with ten or more subjects to teach in a primary school or 400 to teach in a secondary school has time to learn to tell stories themselves. The resources below list various useful sources. But let me first share my approach to learning a story:

a. Choose a story that you enjoy and think the children will enjoy.
b. Read it and sketch a story map to act as a visual reminder of the key scenes.
c. Rewrite the story, simplifying it down to the bare bones. Sometimes I build in key language features that may be at text or sentence level.
d. Hold the map in your hand and pace around, telling the story to yourself – I need somewhere quiet where I am on my own.
e. After a few tellings, a version begins to emerge. The more you tell it, the stronger and more fluent it becomes.
f. Often I make a recording of my version and listen to this in the car. It can help to leave a space between each sentence so that when I am driving along, I hear a sentence and then repeat it in the space. This is very handy for learning simple repetitive stories.
g. When telling a story to a class, it can help to pin up your map or have key incidents on cards if you feel you will need the support. However, if you have told it a number of times to yourself and can really 'see' what happens in your mind then you will be fine. Teachers make good

storytellers because storytelling lies at the heart of good teaching. You do not have to be noisy and showy – a quiet teller can be highly effective.

WHERE TO FIND STORIES FOR TELLING

- *The Bumper Book of Storytelling into Writing: Key Stage 1* and its companion volume *The Bumper Book of Storytelling into Writing: Key Stage 2*, by Pie Corbett (order from Clown Publishing, 7 Ferris Grove, Melksham, Wiltshire SN12 7JW). I wrote both these books to provide an introduction to storytelling. Each book contains a bank of stories for different year groups.
- *The Storymaker's Chest: Key Stage 1* – a treasure chest of a box with puppets, games, an audio CD, cards etc. – the book includes a bank of stories for nursery to year 2.
- Barefoot Books – beautiful traditional tales collections worth buying – in particular, *The Odyssey* retold by Hugh Lupton and Daniel Morden. You can buy both the book and an audio CD. This fabulous retelling brings the tale alive in a way that I have never heard before. It would make a feast for a year 5 or 6 class.
- *The Story Tree* by Hugh Lupton (with an audio CD) – good for Key Stage 1; and *Tales of Wisdom and Wonder* by Hugh Lupton (complete with audio CD). Both from Barefoot Books.
- *Storyteller* – published by Scholastic. This is a series of three anthologies, each with an audio CD, for 4–7 years, 7–9 years and 9–11 years. *Stories by Storytellers*. The three teacher's books each come with a DVD of some of the stories being told by storytellers – Taffy Thomas, Jane Grell, Xanthe Gresham and myself!

If you are in need of more, and catch the storytelling bug, then these books will provide more:

- *Grimm's Fairy Tales* – published by Routledge.

- *Tales from around the World* by Jane Yolen – published by Pantheon.
- *The Magic Lands* retold by Kevin Crossley-Holland – published by Orion.
- *English Fairy Tales*, retold by Joseph Jacobs – Puffin Books.
- *Voyage* – a series of guided readers, selected by Pie Corbett and Chris Buckton – Oxford University Press (one anthology per year across KS2). Short stories for reading and writing.
- *Ready-to-tell-tales* and *More Ready-to-tell tales* – edited by David Holt and Bill Mooney (August House). Excellent resources of Storytellers' Tales for retelling.
- Oxford University Press have a useful series of fairy and traditional tales from around the world.
- *The Story Giant* by Brian Patten (Harper Collins) – an intriguing story about stories.
- For 'Urban Legends', the best and simplest resource is the internet!
- *World Tales* – collected by Idries Shah (Octagon Press) – a great collection from many lands.
- *War with Troy* (Achilles) and *Return from Troy* – great tales retold by Hugh Lupton and Daniel Morden, with excellent CDs and teaching books. Contact Cambridge School Classics Project on 01223 361458. Award winning and inspiring essentials for teaching Greek legends.
- *Telling tales* by Taffy Thomas and Steve Killick – a very good resource book of key tales to develop emotional literacy (01254 882080).

BOOKS AND RESOURCES TO HELP YOU DEVELOP STORYMAKING

- *Traditional Storytelling in the Primary Classroom* – a very handy and practical book by Teresa Grainger – Scholastic.
- Writing workshops: *Teaching Narrative Writing at Key Stage 2* and *Teaching Story Writing at Key Stage 1*, both by Pie Corbett – published by David Fulton Publishers / Routledge. New editions due in 2009.

- *The Story Making Framework* – the original planning framework and account of the research carried out by the International Learning and Research Centre is available by writing to: ILRC, North Street, Oldland Common, South Gloucestershire BS30 8TL.
- *The Storymaker's Chest* – a treasure-trove of story cards, objects, posters etc. Ideal support for telling and writing. There are two chests one for each key stage. These provide the best source of cards – characters, settings, dilemmas, triggers, magic beans, story trails etc. Published by Philip and Tacey.
- *The Story Generator Cube* – quick-fire games using storymaking cards. Great for inventing new stories – Published by Philip and Tacey.
- *Story Mats* – three mats that are graded in difficulty – providing easy-to-use prompts not only for making up stories but also as reminders about varying sentences etc. Published by Philip and Tacey.
- Contact the I.L.R.C. if you would like to train to become a 'storymaking' tutor.
- The Northern Centre for Storytelling in Lakeland – www.taffythomas.co.uk

WEBSITES

Two excellent sites for teachers are:

www.storyarts.org/lessonplans/lessonideas/index.html – lesson ideas and other activities such as treasure hunts.

www.sfs.org.uk – the website of the Society for Storytelling. Also, there are good resources from Hugh Lupton – CDs and tapes that make a fantastic bank of tales for the classroom. There are many links from here into a whole new world of storytelling resources.

THE END STORY

I once heard a story about a man who saw a bee creep out of his girlfriend's mouth while she lay sleeping. That image has haunted me for years. But recently I heard something similar and even more extraordinary from a Norwegian traveller.

This happened years ago, when the villagers were out harvesting the hay. One of the workers noticed a tiny white mouse scuttling about near his girlfriend where she lay sleeping, weary from the morning's work.

Curious, he followed the mouse. It seemed to be trying to cross a little stream. It ran up and down the bank searching for a way across. In the end, the man laid down his scythe across the stream. The mouse ran straight across. On the other side, it scampered up to a grey rock, sniffed round the edges and slipped underneath. A few moments later the mouse reappeared, sniffed the air and then scuttled back over the scythe. The man followed the mouse as it ran straight back towards his girlfriend.

To his amazement it ran up her arm and straight into her mouth. At that moment she awoke, stretched and said 'I've had such a weird dream. I was lost in a green forest until I came to a huge river. I knew that I had to cross it but at first could find no bridge. In the end, I found the strangest bridge made of a long straight wooden plank that led into sharp metal curved like the Moon. On the other side was an enormous grey stone palace. When I had found a small side door, I entered to find it was full of gold and silver. After a while I became afraid so I left, crossed the bridge and ran back home.'

The man took the girl back to the stream and explained what he had seen. They searched around till they found the very stone where the mouse had disappeared. The man lifted the stone and underneath they found buried treasure beyond belief.

May stories become your own treasure that no one can steal.

Pie Corbett
October 2008

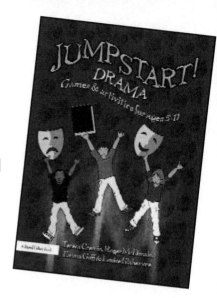

Jumpstart! Poetry

Games and Activities for Ages 7-12

Pie Corbett

A good poetry idea should help the children feel excited about writing and enable them to think of what to write - developing their imagination, creativity and writing skills.

Jumpstart! Poetry is about involving children as creative writers through writing poems. The book contains a bank of ideas that can be drawn upon when teaching poetry but also at other times to provide a source for creative writing that children relish. There are more than 100 quick warm-ups to fire the brain into a creative mood and to 'jumpstart' reading, writing and performing poetry in any key stage 1 or 2 classroom.

Practical, easy-to-do and vastly entertaining, this new 'jumpstart' will appeal to busy teachers in any primary classroom.

September 2008: A5: 200pp
Pb: 978-0-415-46708-7: **£11.99**

For more information on this title visit:
www.routledge.com/teachers